Surviving Cognitive Overload

Reclaiming Your Focus
from Digital Distractions

Surviving Cognitive Overload – Reclaiming Your Focus
from Digital Distractions
Copyright © 2024 by Angel Marqués
All rights reserved.

No part of this book may be reproduced, stored in a retrieval system, or transmitted in any form or by any means—electronic, mechanical, photocopying, recording, or otherwise—without prior written permission from the author, except in the case of brief quotations for book reviews or similar purposes permitted by copyright law.

This is a work of non-fiction. All content and interpretations herein are based on research and analysis by the author. Any resemblance to real persons, living or dead, is purely coincidental.

Published by Angel Marqués Sánchez
ISBN: 9798303815797

Hello! I would greatly appreciate it if you could share your opinion by leaving a review on Amazon. Reviews not only help other readers discover the book, but they're also essential for supporting future projects.

If you have a few minutes, please visit the review page by scanning the QR code below.

THE BATTLE FOR YOUR ATTENTION 5

PART 1: UNDERSTANDING THE ATTENTION ECONOMY ... 17

The Business of Attention 18

Exploiting Human Vulnerabilities 37

The Rise of Cognitive Overload 60

PART 2: THE HUMAN COST OF COGNITIVE OVERLOAD ... 75

Neurological Consequences 76

Integration of Effects: The Cumulative Toll 84

The Decline of Deep Thinking 94

Societal Implications 115

PART 3: RECLAIMING YOUR FOCUS 125

The Mindful Technology User 126

Cultivating Attention and Focus 137

Designing a Healthier 152

DISCOVER MORE 175

The Battle for Your Attention

You wake up to the shrill ping of your phone, the glow of its screen pulling you from sleep before your feet even touch the floor. Notifications await—a cascade of emails, news alerts, messages, and updates. Each one demands your attention, a small tether pulling you further into the digital sphere. Over breakfast, you scroll through headlines and social media feeds, filling the quiet moments with information and noise. Hours later, you find yourself lying in bed again, the screen still illuminating your face, your mind buzzing with fragments of the day's relentless stream of content. This is the modern reality for billions—a life punctuated by the hum of notifications and the never-ending scroll.

The battle for attention defines our era, a silent but ferocious war waged by corporations, platforms, and algorithms. Globally, the digital advertising industry has ballooned into a $600 billion behemoth, a testament to the immense value of your focus. Every second you spend on a screen, every click, every like, every pause is meticulously tracked, analyzed, and monetized. Attention has become the ultimate commodity, bought and sold with ruthless precision. And yet, as this economy flourishes, its impact on the human mind remains poorly understood, a shadow looming over our collective future.

In this environment, the concept of cognitive overload has become more than a personal affliction—it is a defining feature of modern life. Cognitive overload occurs when the volume of information we are exposed to surpasses our brain's capacity to process it effectively. It is the sensation of being stretched too thin, the inability to focus deeply or think clearly, the creeping exhaustion that follows days spent cycling through endless updates, alerts, and stimuli. This isn't merely a side effect of technology but a direct consequence of systems designed to keep us perpetually distracted. Social media platforms, news outlets, and entertainment services rely on a barrage of interruptions, exploiting our psychological vulnerabilities to keep us engaged.

But this crisis of attention did not emerge overnight. For centuries, technological advances have shaped how humans process information and interact with the world. The printing press made knowledge widely available, but it also overwhelmed early readers with the sudden abundance of books. The telegraph introduced real-time communication, collapsing distances and reshaping how societies understood time itself. Each new innovation brought with it both progress and disruption. What sets today apart is the speed and scale at which these changes occur. The smartphone, only a decade and a half old, has transformed human behavior more radically than most inventions in human history. Where previous shifts unfolded over generations, the digital revolution has taken place within a single lifetime.

This constant exposure to stimulation is not just tiring—it is reshaping us. Our ability to focus for long periods, to think critically, to reflect deeply is eroding. Creativity falters in the face of endless distractions, and boredom—once a fertile ground for innovation—has all but disappeared. Neurologically, our brains are struggling to keep up. The dopamine-driven cycle of likes, shares, and notifications rewires our neural pathways, making us more reactive and less reflective. The long-term consequences are only beginning to reveal themselves, but already we see the toll: rising anxiety, fractured attention, and an increasing inability to sustain meaningful relationships or engage with complex ideas.

Yet, this is not just a personal struggle—it is a societal one. As individuals, we may feel the effects of cognitive overload in our daily lives, but collectively, the stakes are even higher. Democracies falter when public discourse becomes fragmented and shallow. Social cohesion erodes when empathy is overshadowed by outrage. The challenges of the 21st century—climate change, inequality, global health—require sustained focus and collaborative effort, but the attention economy pushes us in the opposite direction.

So, how did we get here? How has attention, once a personal resource, become the most valuable currency of the digital age? What is this doing to our minds, our relationships, our societies? And most importantly, how do we fight back? This book is not about rejecting technology—it is about reclaiming our autonomy within it. It is about learning to navigate a world designed to distract us without losing sight of what truly matters. In the pages that follow, we will uncover the mechanisms of cognitive overload, examine its profound consequences, and explore strategies to regain control over our focus and, ultimately, our lives. This is not just a survival guide for the digital age—it is a call to rediscover the art of attention.

Cognitive overload is not a new concept, though its manifestations have grown more acute and pervasive in the modern era. At the very essence, it describes a fundamental human limitation: the finite capacity of our brains to process information. Just as a cup can only hold so much water before it overflows, our cognitive systems are designed to handle a finite amount of stimuli, tasks, and decisions at any given time. When this threshold is exceeded, the result is mental fatigue, confusion, and an inability to function optimally. In a world where information is abundant but attention is scarce, cognitive overload has become an unavoidable byproduct of contemporary life.

This phenomenon is not just an individual burden but a structural condition, woven into the very fabric of our digital environment. Technology, which once promised to simplify our lives, now saturates them with complexity. Social media platforms, search engines, and news aggregators are not neutral tools but sophisticated systems designed to extract and hold attention. Every notification, trending topic, and algorithmic recommendation adds to the flood of stimuli competing for our focus. The result is a perpetual state of distraction, where our cognitive capacities are constantly stretched thin.

But what makes cognitive overload so insidious is its ability to operate invisibly. Unlike physical exhaustion, which we can easily recognize and address, the mental strain of processing endless streams of information often goes unnoticed until it manifests as burnout, anxiety, or a pervasive sense of being overwhelmed. It is the background hum of modern existence, an ever-present pressure that we rarely stop to question. Why, for instance, do we feel the need to check our phones dozens, even hundreds of times a day? Why do we instinctively reach for our devices during moments of stillness or boredom? The answers lie in the deliberate exploitation of psychological vulnerabilities by those who design our digital experiences.

Central to this exploitation is the concept of intermittent reinforcement, a behavioral mechanism that rewards us unpredictably and keeps us coming back for more. Likes on a photo, comments on a post, or the thrill of discovering something new in an endless scroll all tap into the same neural pathways that make gambling so addictive. This cycle of unpredictable rewards not only captures our attention but also fragments it, pulling us from one stimulus to the next without allowing for sustained focus or deep thought.

The consequences of this constant stimulation are profound. At a neurological level, our brains are being rewired, favoring short bursts of engagement over prolonged concentration. Research shows that multitasking, often celebrated as a modern skill, actually reduces efficiency and increases cognitive load. Tasks take longer, errors multiply, and the quality of work diminishes. On a psychological level, the inability to focus deeply undermines our sense of accomplishment and creativity. Instead of solving problems or generating new ideas, we find ourselves trapped in cycles of shallow engagement, flitting from one distraction to the next.

Cognitive overload also carries social implications, eroding our ability to connect meaningfully with others. Relationships require attention—undivided, sustained, and intentional focus. Yet, in a world where every moment is interrupted by pings and alerts, giving someone our full attention has become a rarity. The same applies to our engagement with larger societal issues. Addressing complex challenges like climate change or social inequality requires deep thinking and sustained effort, yet our collective attention is scattered, diverted by the endless churn of news cycles and online debates.

Understanding cognitive overload, then, is not just about recognizing its effects but also about interrogating the systems that perpetuate it. It is about asking why our environments are designed to overwhelm us and whose interests this serves. It is about reclaiming our cognitive autonomy in the face of forces that seek to commodify our attention. Above all, it is about recognizing that while the problem may feel deeply personal, it is also deeply structural, demanding both individual and collective responses.

As we delve deeper into this book, we will unpack the mechanisms that fuel cognitive overload, examine the toll it takes on our minds and societies, and explore strategies for resisting its pull. The goal is not to escape the modern world but to navigate it with intention, clarity, and a renewed sense of agency. In doing so, we can begin to shift the balance of power in the attention economy, reclaiming our focus not just for ourselves but for the people, ideas, and causes that matter most.

The story of cognitive overload is not a phenomenon unique to the digital age. It is, instead, the latest chapter in a long history of humanity's relationship with information, one shaped by successive technological revolutions that have continually redefined how we think, communicate, and process the world around us. To understand how we arrived at this moment—where attention itself is commodified and our cognitive capacities are under siege—we must first look back and trace the evolution of information and its impact on human life.

Centuries ago, the invention of the printing press in the 15th century marked a seismic shift in how knowledge was produced and disseminated. For the first time, books could be mass-produced, unleashing an unprecedented flood of information. What was once scarce and precious—written knowledge—suddenly became abundant, and for many, overwhelming. Scholars of the time expressed concerns that this "information explosion" might lead to confusion rather than enlightenment, as readers struggled to keep up with the sheer volume of texts available to them. In hindsight, the printing press was not only the beginning of modern information culture but also the first instance of humanity grappling with cognitive overload on a large scale.

Fast forward to the 19th century, and the telegraph brought another revolution. For the first time in human history, messages could travel faster than the speed of physical movement, collapsing time and space in ways that radically altered the flow of information. News from distant lands arrived in an instant, and with it came the constant pressure to stay updated. By the early 20th century, the rise of mass media—newspapers, radio, and later television—amplified this trend, creating a world in which information was not only more accessible but also more curated and commodified. Each of these innovations brought undeniable progress, but they also introduced new challenges for the human mind, which had to adapt to processing increasingly complex and abundant streams of data.

The digital revolution of the late 20th century intensified these dynamics exponentially. The advent of personal computers, the internet, and eventually smartphones transformed information into something omnipresent, accessible at any time and from anywhere. Where previous eras had limits—books needed to be physically printed, newspapers arrived only once a day, and television programs aired on fixed schedules—the digital age erased those boundaries. Information became not just abundant but infinite, a ceaseless torrent that follows us everywhere we go. At the heart of this shift lies the attention economy, a system in which our focus is not merely a byproduct of engagement but a resource to be extracted, manipulated, and monetized.

What distinguishes the digital age from previous revolutions is not just the volume of information but the precision with which it is delivered. Algorithmic curation, powered by artificial intelligence, ensures that each individual's feed, notifications, and recommendations are uniquely tailored to capture and hold their attention. Platforms learn our preferences, predict our behaviors, and serve us content designed to maximize engagement. Unlike the printing press or the telegraph, today's technologies do not passively provide information; they actively shape what we see, think, and feel.

Yet, as revolutionary as these tools are, they also prey on vulnerabilities that are deeply rooted in human psychology. The same instincts that once helped us survive—our attraction to novelty, our sensitivity to threats, our desire for social validation—are now exploited by systems that encourage endless scrolling, constant checking, and perpetual distraction. What began as a means of enhancing knowledge and connection has, in many cases, become a mechanism for overloading our cognitive capacities and fragmenting our focus.

This historical trajectory reveals an uncomfortable truth: cognitive overload is not an accident or an inevitable consequence of technological progress. It is a structural outcome of systems designed to prioritize profit over well-being, engagement over understanding, and immediacy over depth. By looking back, we can see how each technological leap brought with it both opportunities and challenges, and how, with each step, the balance has shifted further toward the commodification of attention.

Understanding this history is crucial because it reminds us that the present is not immutable. The forces that shape our relationship with technology—and, by extension, with ourselves—are not beyond our control. If the printing press and the telegraph brought cognitive challenges that we eventually learned to manage, then the same can be true for the digital age. But this requires more than passive adaptation; it demands active, deliberate choices about how we engage with the technologies that define our lives.

As we move forward in this exploration, we will delve deeper into the unique pressures of our time, but we do so with the knowledge that our current struggles are part of a larger, ongoing narrative. The question is not whether we can live with technology but whether we can learn to live well despite its demands. Only by understanding the past can we hope to chart a path toward a more balanced and intentional future.

The effects of cognitive overload ripple through every corner of our lives, shaping not only our individual well-being but also the structures of our societies. At first glance, the impact may seem subtle, almost invisible—a nagging inability to concentrate, a vague sense of fatigue. But as the cumulative strain mounts, the true costs become impossible to ignore. On a personal level, cognitive overload diminishes our mental health, fractures our relationships, and erodes our capacity for creativity and deep thinking. On a societal level, it undermines collective action, weakens democratic institutions, and threatens the very fabric of our shared humanity.

At the heart of the personal cost lies our overstimulated minds. Constant exposure to notifications, messages, and algorithmically curated feeds prevents the brain from entering states of sustained focus. Tasks that once required deep concentration now feel insurmountable, as our attention flits from one stimulus to the next, always craving the next hit of novelty. Neurologically, this relentless cycle reshapes our brains, reinforcing habits of reactivity over reflection.

Dopamine pathways—the same mechanisms that drive addiction—are hijacked, leaving us increasingly dependent on short bursts of gratification while our ability to engage in prolonged, meaningful thought diminishes.

The consequences for mental health are profound. Anxiety and stress, fueled by the constant barrage of information, have become defining features of modern life. Decision fatigue—the result of making countless trivial choices, from what to watch to which email to prioritize—leaves us feeling depleted, unable to muster the energy for more significant decisions. Sleep, a cornerstone of mental and physical health, is often the first casualty, as the glow of screens and the pull of endless content encroach on our nights. Over time, these effects compound, creating a pervasive sense of disconnection—not only from others but also from ourselves.

This disconnection extends beyond the individual to our relationships. Genuine human connection demands presence, the ability to listen, empathize, and engage without distraction. Yet, in a world where attention is fragmented, such presence is increasingly rare. Conversations are punctuated by glances at phones, family dinners compete with digital interruptions, and even moments of intimacy are diluted by the ever-present hum of the online world. Over time, this erosion of attention undermines the bonds that hold relationships together, replacing depth with superficiality.

On a societal level, the consequences are no less alarming. Democracies rely on informed and engaged citizens, capable of critical thinking and deliberation. But the attention economy, with its emphasis on speed and sensationalism, fosters the opposite: a populace overwhelmed by fragmented information, prone to emotional reactions, and unable to sustain focus on complex issues. Political discourse becomes shallow and polarized, driven by outrage and misinformation rather than reasoned debate. Collective challenges, from climate change to economic inequality, demand sustained focus and collaboration—yet these qualities are precisely what cognitive overload undermines.

The economic structures that fuel the attention economy exacerbate these societal costs. Platforms profit by keeping us engaged, regardless of the consequences for our well-being or social cohesion. Algorithms are optimized not for truth or understanding but for clicks and shares, creating echo chambers that reinforce biases and deepen divisions. The result is a society that feels increasingly fragmented, its shared realities replaced by competing narratives tailored to individual preferences.

Yet perhaps the most insidious cost of cognitive overload is the erosion of our humanity. To be human is to create, to reflect, to connect, and to aspire. These capacities require time, attention, and mental space—resources that are increasingly scarce in the modern world. When our lives are governed by the demands of an attention economy, we risk becoming passive participants, shaped more by external forces than by our own intentions. We lose the ability to ask the deeper questions: What kind of life do we want to live? What kind of society do we want to build?

Understanding the personal and societal costs of cognitive overload is not an exercise in despair but a call to action. It is an invitation to recognize the stakes of this moment and to reclaim what has been lost. The question is not just how to survive in this environment but how to resist its pull and rediscover the values that make life meaningful. As we confront these challenges, we must remember that the battle for our attention is also a battle for our humanity—and it is one we cannot afford to lose.

Fighting back against the forces that drive cognitive overload requires more than superficial adjustments or fleeting moments of mindfulness. It demands a fundamental shift in how we think about attention, technology, and our relationship with the world. This is not a battle to reject modernity or retreat from the digital sphere entirely, but rather an effort to reclaim our agency and reshape the systems that have come to dominate our lives. To fight back is to recognize that attention is not just a resource—it is a foundation of identity, creativity, and connection. By taking deliberate steps to protect it, we can restore balance to both our personal lives and the broader social structures that rely on a focused, engaged populace.

At the personal level, the first act of resistance is awareness. Cognitive overload thrives on invisibility; its effects often go unnoticed until they manifest as exhaustion, anxiety, or dissatisfaction. By consciously observing how our attention is spent—what captures it, what drains it, and what enriches it—we begin to see the patterns that shape our days. This awareness allows us to make intentional choices, to question whether the time spent scrolling through endless feeds or reacting to constant notifications aligns with our values and goals. The act of pausing, of asking why we are drawn to certain behaviors, disrupts the cycle of mindless engagement that fuels the attention economy.

Mindfulness practices can serve as powerful tools in this fight, not as a panacea but as a means of recalibrating our relationship with distraction. Through meditation, journaling, or simply taking moments of stillness, we can train our minds to resist the pull of external stimuli and cultivate an inner space of calm and focus. These practices, however, are only part of the solution. Mindfulness must extend beyond individual effort to influence the environments in which we live and work. Without structural changes, personal strategies risk becoming mere coping mechanisms in a system designed to overwhelm.

On a structural level, fighting back means advocating for a reimagining of the technologies that shape our world. The platforms and devices that monopolize our attention are not immutable; they are products of choices made by designers, developers, and corporations. By demanding greater accountability from these entities, we can push for ethical design practices that prioritize user well-being over engagement metrics. Features like customizable notification settings, screen-time management tools, and algorithmic transparency represent small but meaningful steps toward creating a digital landscape that serves people rather than exploiting them.

Policy and regulation also have a critical role to play. Governments can and should intervene to curb the most harmful practices of the attention economy, much as they have done in other industries that impact public health. Advertising restrictions, data privacy laws, and measures to combat misinformation are not about stifling innovation but about ensuring that technological progress aligns with human flourishing. These interventions, however, must be informed by a nuanced understanding of both technology and human behavior, avoiding the pitfalls of overly simplistic or reactionary measures.

Collectively, we must also reclaim the cultural narratives that celebrate distraction and multitasking as signs of productivity and success. Deep work, sustained focus, and meaningful engagement should not be seen as outdated virtues but as essential skills for navigating an increasingly complex world. This cultural shift begins with education, teaching not only children but also adults how to manage their attention in a digital age. Schools and workplaces can play a vital role, fostering environments that support concentration and discourage the constant interruptions that have become the norm.

We must reimagine our relationship with time itself. The rhythms of modern life often leave little room for reflection, creativity, or rest, perpetuating the cycle of overload. By prioritizing quality over quantity—whether in our work, our relationships, or our consumption of information—we can begin to create lives that feel less hurried and more meaningful. This is not about doing less but about doing what matters, about investing our attention in ways that align with our deepest values and aspirations.

Fighting back against cognitive overload is not a solitary endeavor. It is a collective challenge that requires both individual and systemic change. But it is also an opportunity—a chance to reassert control over our lives, to reconnect with what is truly important, and to build a society that values focus, depth, and connection over endless distraction. The battle for our attention is not just about resisting the forces that seek to exploit it; it is about reclaiming the essence of who we are. To fight back is to choose presence over passivity, intention over impulse, and meaning over mindlessness. It is, ultimately, an act of hope.

Part 1: Understanding the Attention Economy

The Business of Attention

The concept of the attention economy emerges from a fundamental truth about human cognition: our capacity to focus is limited, while the demands on that focus have grown exponentially. In the mid-twentieth century, economist and psychologist Herbert A. Simon famously articulated that "a wealth of information creates a poverty of attention," a prescient observation that resonates more strongly today than ever before. The digital age has amplified this reality, transforming attention from a natural, intangible human function into a scarce commodity with immense market value. It is no longer just what we attend to that matters, but how long we can sustain that attention and how deeply it engages us. This commodification of attention has birthed an entire economy, where corporations compete to capture and monetize our focus, often at the expense of our mental and emotional well-being.

At the heart of the attention economy lies the profound shift in how value is generated. Traditional economic systems relied on tangible goods and services, transactions with clear boundaries. In contrast, the attention economy thrives on intangibility—it is not about what you purchase but how you spend your time. Platforms like Facebook, YouTube, and Instagram, ostensibly free for users, have mastered the art of making attention the product. Every moment spent scrolling, clicking, or watching feeds into a meticulously designed system that transforms engagement into revenue. This is not a passive process; it is a deeply strategic one, underpinned by algorithms engineered to maximize the time users remain captive. Every "like," every notification, and every curated recommendation is a calculated attempt to keep you looking just a little longer.

The shift to an attention-based model has been nothing short of revolutionary. Advertising, once confined to static spaces like billboards or magazine pages, has become a dynamic, pervasive force that follows users across digital landscapes. Unlike traditional media, where the success of an advertisement was measured in estimates and projections, digital platforms offer granular data about every click, hover, and pause. This granular tracking allows companies to deliver personalized ads with uncanny accuracy, making each moment of attention more valuable than ever before. The rise of this hyper-targeted advertising has made platforms immensely profitable; companies like Meta and Alphabet generate billions annually, their business models dependent on the simple act of users paying attention.

Yet, the attention economy is not merely a matter of dollars and data. It is an economic system that thrives on exploiting human psychology, leveraging our vulnerabilities to ensure we remain engaged. The very architecture of these platforms is designed to foster dependency, exploiting innate cognitive tendencies such as the human preference for novelty and the psychological hooks of intermittent reinforcement. This system does not simply respond to our desires; it shapes them, guiding behaviors in ways that align with corporate interests while often undermining individual agency. This tension—between what platforms promise as tools for connection or entertainment and their role as engines of profit—defines the paradox of the attention economy.

The implications of this shift are profound, extending far beyond individual users. In many ways, the attention economy reshapes the fabric of society itself, influencing how we communicate, consume information, and prioritize what matters. The stakes are not merely personal but collective, as the ability to direct attention becomes critical for addressing the most pressing issues of our time. The attention economy, therefore, is not just a modern challenge; it is a defining feature of contemporary life, one that demands a deeper understanding if we are to navigate its complexities and reclaim the autonomy it so persistently seeks to erode.

How Platforms Capture Attention

The mechanisms by which platforms capture attention are neither accidental nor benign; they are the result of meticulous design rooted in a sophisticated understanding of human behavior. At the core of these systems lies the algorithm, a complex set of instructions crafted to predict, influence, and ultimately monopolize user focus. Unlike traditional content delivery, where users actively choose what they wish to engage with, these algorithms curate an endless stream of personalized material, making every interaction feel tailored and relevant. This personalization is not merely a feature but a strategy. It ensures that the content delivered aligns with the user's preferences, habits, and even emotional state, reducing the likelihood of disengagement and fostering a sense of seamless immersion.

One of the most effective tools in this arsenal is the infinite scroll. This seemingly innocuous feature, pioneered by platforms like Facebook and Twitter, removes natural stopping points, encouraging users to continue consuming content without pause. It exploits the psychological principle of the "variable reward system," where the anticipation of finding something rewarding—perhaps a funny video, a breaking news story, or a friend's post—keeps users glued to their screens. Unlike finite activities, such as reading a book or watching a movie, the infinite scroll creates the illusion that something better is always just a flick away, trapping users in a cycle of perpetual seeking.

Notifications, too, play a pivotal role in the attention-capturing arsenal. These seemingly simple alerts are strategically designed to interrupt and redirect focus, leveraging the brain's sensitivity to novelty and urgency. A red badge, a buzzing phone, or a subtle vibration triggers a response that is both psychological and physiological, activating the brain's reward centers with the promise of something important or gratifying. This interruption is not passive; it reshapes attention patterns, pulling users back into the platform even when they have no conscious intention of engaging. Over time, these notifications condition users to check their devices compulsively, fostering a dependency that benefits the platform while subtly eroding the user's ability to concentrate on other tasks.

Beyond these overt strategies, platforms employ subtler techniques that capitalize on social and emotional instincts. The use of "likes," comments, and shares taps into the human need for social validation, creating a feedback loop where users seek acknowledgment and approval through digital interaction. The drive to share experiences or opinions becomes less about authentic connection and more about accruing social capital within the ecosystem of the platform. This manipulation of social instincts transforms natural behaviors into quantifiable metrics, each one furthering the platform's ability to hold attention and drive engagement.

Perhaps most insidious is the illusion of agency that these platforms cultivate. Users believe they are making free choices about what to watch, read, or explore, when in reality, their options are curated and constrained by algorithms designed to prioritize profit over authenticity. The content they see is not a reflection of the world as it is, but a calculated selection meant to maximize their time and attention on the platform. In this way, the mechanisms of attention capture not only shape individual behaviors but also influence collective realities, blurring the line between voluntary engagement and involuntary manipulation. This engineered environment raises pressing ethical questions about autonomy, consent, and the true cost of a system that profits from the commodification of human attention.

FROM ENGAGEMENT TO REVENUE

The journey from user engagement to revenue generation is a masterclass in transforming human attention into economic capital. Platforms have perfected the art of monetizing the moments we spend scrolling, liking, or watching, converting our time into a commodity as valuable as oil in the digital economy. This transformation hinges on the intricate interplay of data collection, targeted advertising, and behavioral manipulation, creating a self-perpetuating cycle that enriches corporations while leaving users increasingly entangled in their systems.

At the heart of this revenue model lies data—the digital footprints users leave behind with every click, search, or interaction. Platforms like Facebook, YouTube, and Twitter operate as sophisticated surveillance systems, collecting vast quantities of information about user behavior, preferences, and demographics. This data is then processed by advanced algorithms to construct detailed profiles, offering advertisers unparalleled insights into their target audiences. The precision of this profiling is what makes these platforms so lucrative, as businesses can tailor their ads to reach not just broad demographics, but individuals whose behaviors suggest a high likelihood of engagement and conversion.

Targeted advertising is the linchpin of this process, enabling platforms to charge premium rates for access to their finely segmented user bases. Unlike traditional media advertising, which casts a wide net in the hope of capturing a small percentage of interested viewers, digital advertising ensures that every ad reaches someone whose data suggests they are a potential customer. For example, an individual who has recently searched for running shoes might find their social media feed inundated with advertisements for athletic gear, fitness trackers, and local running clubs. This hyper-relevance makes digital advertising incredibly effective, driving higher engagement rates and justifying the enormous sums companies invest in these platforms.

The engagement-revenue loop is further reinforced by the very design of these platforms, which prioritize content that keeps users interacting for as long as possible. Algorithms favor posts and videos that provoke emotional responses—whether delight, outrage, or curiosity—because heightened emotions increase the likelihood of likes, shares, and comments. This engagement, in turn, generates more data, which refines the algorithms and enhances the platform's ability to serve precisely targeted ads. In this feedback loop, user engagement is not just a byproduct of the platform's design but its primary engine of profitability.

Subscription models and premium services add another layer to the revenue strategy. Platforms like YouTube Premium or Spotify monetize attention not only through ads but also by offering users an escape from them—for a price. This dual approach ensures that every user, regardless of whether they pay directly or indirectly, contributes to the platform's revenue stream. Even those who opt out of subscriptions often find themselves nudged toward longer engagement times through features like autoplay, which seamlessly transitions from one piece of content to the next, reducing the chances of disengagement.

Perhaps the most profound aspect of this system is how it shapes not just individual behavior but the broader digital ecosystem. By tying revenue to engagement, platforms have a vested interest in promoting content and features that maximize attention, often at the expense of user well-being or societal cohesion. The economic imperative to keep users scrolling overrides considerations of truth, mental health, or public discourse, creating a digital landscape where profit, rather than value or ethics, dictates the flow of information. This commodification of attention, while immensely profitable for a select few, raises critical questions about its long-term implications for users, societies, and even democracies.

The Cost of Free Platforms

The allure of free platforms, offering access to global communities, endless entertainment, and real-time information, masks a far more insidious truth: nothing comes without a cost. In the digital economy, the adage "If you're not paying for the product, you are the product" rings particularly true. Platforms like Facebook, YouTube, and TikTok have revolutionized the way we connect and consume content, but the price we pay is not monetary—it is the surrender of our attention, privacy, and, often, our well-being.

The cost begins with the relentless extraction of user data, which is not merely incidental but foundational to the business models of free platforms. Every interaction, whether it's a like, a click, or a pause on a particular video, is meticulously tracked, analyzed, and stored. These platforms do not just observe behavior—they anticipate it. Sophisticated algorithms learn to predict user preferences with startling accuracy, creating profiles that are sold to advertisers in real time. This exchange, where users unknowingly trade their data for access, underpins the "free" experience but also normalizes surveillance as an inescapable feature of modern life.

The implications extend beyond privacy. The design of free platforms is inherently exploitative, prioritizing engagement above all else. Algorithms are optimized not for user satisfaction but for time spent on the platform, ensuring a steady flow of ad impressions. This has a profound psychological impact, as users are drawn into cycles of dopamine-driven engagement, whether through the excitement of a viral video, the validation of likes, or the outrage provoked by inflammatory content. What begins as a harmless distraction often evolves into a dependency, eroding the capacity for sustained focus and critical thinking.

Moreover, the cost of free platforms is disproportionately borne by users who lack awareness of these mechanisms or the resources to mitigate their effects. Children, for instance, are particularly vulnerable to the addictive qualities of these platforms, as their developing brains are less equipped to navigate the engineered feedback loops of notifications and rewards. Similarly, marginalized communities often become the targets of misinformation campaigns, predatory advertising, or algorithmic biases, highlighting the ethical concerns inherent in systems that prioritize profit over equity.

The societal costs are equally alarming. The monetization of attention incentivizes the spread of sensationalism, misinformation, and polarizing content, fracturing public discourse and undermining trust in institutions. News sites reliant on advertising revenue are compelled to prioritize clickbait headlines over investigative journalism, while social media platforms amplify divisive narratives to maximize engagement. This creates an environment where the pursuit of truth is secondary to the pursuit of clicks, leaving users not only misinformed but increasingly isolated in echo chambers designed to reaffirm existing biases.

Even at an environmental level, the cost of free platforms is staggering. The energy required to power data centers, store user information, and process algorithmic calculations contributes significantly to the carbon footprint of the digital economy. While users enjoy the convenience of endless content at their fingertips, the ecological toll of maintaining these systems remains largely hidden, raising questions about the sustainability of a model that prioritizes constant growth and engagement.

Free platforms, then, are anything but free. They exact a toll on individuals, societies, and the planet, leveraging the illusion of costlessness to perpetuate a system of exploitation and dependency. While these platforms offer undeniable benefits—connecting distant friends, democratizing access to information, and enabling creative expression—the hidden costs demand scrutiny. Recognizing these trade-offs is the first step toward reclaiming autonomy and fostering a more ethical digital landscape, where the benefits of technology are balanced against its profound and often unseen consequences.

GLOBAL PERSPECTIVE

The phenomenon of attention commodification is not confined to a single culture or society; it is a global enterprise with far-reaching implications. Platforms like Facebook, Google, and TikTok operate across continents, adapting their strategies to tap into local markets while maintaining a singular focus on maximizing engagement. This universality of the attention economy has made it a cultural force, shaping the ways people interact with technology and with each other, regardless of geography. However, the global nature of this phenomenon also amplifies its risks and inequities, reflecting the stark contrasts in how different societies experience its benefits and burdens.

In developed nations, where high-speed internet and ubiquitous smartphones are the norm, the attention economy thrives in environments of technological saturation. Here, platforms capitalize on the wealth of data generated by constant connectivity, creating deeply personalized experiences designed to hook users for longer periods. But this comes at a cost: mental health crises linked to digital addiction, rising rates of anxiety, and declining attention spans. The economic powerhouses of the attention economy, such as the United States and China, have become epicenters of these issues, with their citizens caught in a paradox of technological empowerment and cognitive exploitation.

In emerging economies, the dynamics are different but no less significant. For many in regions like Africa, South Asia, or Latin America, platforms serve as gateways to the digital world, offering opportunities for connection, education, and economic growth. Initiatives like Facebook's Free Basics or Google's low-cost Android devices have introduced millions to the internet, ostensibly with the noble aim of bridging the digital divide. Yet these efforts are far from altruistic; they embed users into ecosystems that prioritize corporate interests. Free access to specific platforms often comes at the expense of open access to the broader internet, funneling users into spaces where their attention and data can be monetized most effectively.

Cultural contexts further complicate the global reach of the attention economy. In regions with strong communal traditions, platforms often reshape how communities interact, sometimes disrupting long-standing social norms. The dominance of globalized content can overshadow local voices, eroding cultural diversity in favor of homogenized, algorithmically preferred narratives. Meanwhile, in politically repressive regimes, the mechanisms of the attention economy are weaponized, with platforms facilitating state surveillance and the spread of propaganda. The very tools designed to connect and empower are often co-opted to control and manipulate, particularly in contexts where democratic safeguards are weak.

Global inequalities also manifest in how the economic benefits of the attention economy are distributed. While tech giants reap enormous profits, many of the regions generating the data that drives this wealth see little return. For example, the vast user bases in India or Brazil contribute to the bottom lines of Silicon Valley firms, but these nations often lack the regulatory frameworks to ensure fair distribution of economic gains. This asymmetry mirrors broader patterns of digital colonialism, where the resources of the Global South—now in the form of data and attention—are extracted to fuel the prosperity of the Global North.

Yet, the global nature of the attention economy also provides a foundation for collective resistance. Around the world, movements are emerging to challenge the dominance of attention-capturing platforms. In Europe, regulatory initiatives like the General Data Protection Regulation (GDPR) have sought to curtail the excesses of data exploitation. In Asia, digital literacy campaigns aim to educate users about the hidden costs of free platforms. Even in countries with minimal regulation, grassroots efforts to promote mindful technology use and alternative platforms are gaining traction, reflecting a growing awareness of the need to reclaim autonomy over attention.

Ultimately, the global perspective on the attention economy reveals a complex interplay of opportunity and exploitation, empowerment and dependency. While technology has undeniably bridged gaps and created possibilities that were once unimaginable, its universal reach necessitates a universal reckoning. Only by addressing the disparities and challenges inherent in this system can we begin to envision a future where the benefits of the digital age are equitably shared, and the costs are borne not by the most vulnerable but by the architects of the system itself.

Ethical and Societal Impacts

The ethical and societal implications of the attention economy are profound, raising urgent questions about the long-term consequences of commodifying human focus. Deep down, the attention economy operates on a business model that prioritizes engagement above all else, often at the expense of individual well-being, social cohesion, and even democratic integrity. The ethical dilemmas it poses are not just abstract concerns but pressing issues that touch nearly every facet of modern life, from mental health to the quality of public discourse.

One of the most troubling aspects of this system is its exploitation of psychological vulnerabilities. By leveraging insights from behavioral psychology, platforms have created environments that are not merely addictive but intentionally designed to manipulate user behavior. Features like infinite scrolling, autoplay, and algorithmic recommendations are crafted to maximize time spent on a platform, disregarding the potential harm to mental health. This raises ethical concerns about consent and agency. Are users truly making free choices when every aspect of their digital experience is engineered to keep them engaged, often at the expense of their well-being? The normalization of such tactics has created a culture where manipulation is not only accepted but celebrated as innovation.

Beyond the individual, the societal impacts are equally alarming. The prioritization of engagement has led to the amplification of sensational, divisive, and often false content. Algorithms that reward extreme emotions—be it outrage, fear, or indignation—have fundamentally reshaped public discourse, fostering polarization and eroding trust in institutions. In this environment, nuanced discussion and critical thinking are overshadowed by the viral appeal of oversimplified narratives and conspiracy theories. The result is not just a fragmented society but one increasingly vulnerable to misinformation and manipulation, with significant consequences for democratic processes and collective decision-making.

The ethical implications extend to questions of equity and representation. The attention economy, driven by algorithms, often perpetuates existing biases and inequities. Marginalized voices are frequently drowned out, while harmful stereotypes and discriminatory practices are reinforced by systems that prioritize engagement over fairness. For instance, studies have shown that algorithms are more likely to surface content that aligns with dominant cultural norms, sidelining diverse perspectives. This digital inequity reflects broader societal injustices, raising critical questions about the responsibility of tech companies to promote inclusivity and equity.

Children and adolescents are particularly vulnerable to the ethical failings of the attention economy. Growing up in a world dominated by digital engagement, they are exposed to platforms that prioritize profit over their developmental needs. The long-term consequences of this exposure—on attention spans, social skills, and mental health—are only beginning to be understood. That platforms knowingly target young users with addictive features and monetized content adds a disturbing layer to the ethical critique, highlighting the need for stricter regulation and accountability.

Despite these challenges, the attention economy also holds the potential for positive societal change, provided its architects take ethical responsibility seriously. Platforms have the capacity to amplify educational content, foster global connections, and drive collective action on critical issues like climate change and social justice. However, realizing this potential requires a fundamental shift in priorities—from maximizing profit to maximizing societal benefit. Ethical technology design, transparent algorithms, and meaningful user consent must become central tenets of the digital ecosystem.

The societal implications of the attention economy demand a reevaluation of what it means to create and consume technology ethically. As users, policymakers, and technologists grapple with these challenges, the focus must shift from treating attention as a commodity to recognizing it as a shared human resource. The ethical questions posed by the attention economy are not merely about the choices of individuals but about the kind of society we wish to build in an increasingly digital world. This is not just a debate about technology; it is a debate about values, justice, and the collective future of humanity.

Algorithmic Influence

Algorithms are mathematical formulas designed to process data and deliver outcomes. However, in the context of the digital world, they have evolved far beyond mere tools for sorting and organizing information. They have become architects of our experiences, shaping what we see, read, and interact with in ways that are often invisible to us. When you open your favorite social media app, scroll through a streaming service, or check the latest news on an aggregator site, algorithms are at work, quietly and systematically tailoring the content to hold your attention. These processes are not neutral; they are finely tuned mechanisms designed to achieve one purpose above all else: engagement. Every click, like, share, or pause feeds into these systems, enabling them to learn your preferences and adapt their output accordingly. Over time, they become increasingly skilled at delivering what you are most likely to consume, creating an experience that feels personalized and, consequently, difficult to step away from.

What makes this system so powerful is its ability to adapt and evolve in real-time. Unlike static programming, algorithms can analyze vast amounts of behavioral data and refine their predictions with every interaction. They learn not just what you explicitly express interest in but also what you unconsciously gravitate toward. The speed and precision with which they operate give them an almost uncanny ability to predict and influence user behavior. When you linger on a video or revisit a particular type of content, the algorithm notices, recalibrates, and adjusts its suggestions to draw you in even further. This iterative process is designed to create a sense of seamlessness, where each piece of content feels like a natural progression from the last. In reality, it is a carefully curated experience meant to keep you engaged for as long as possible.

The influence of algorithms extends beyond individual users, shaping entire communities and even societal trends. As they prioritize engagement, algorithms often amplify content that triggers emotional responses—whether it's outrage, joy, or fear. These emotions drive interaction, and interaction feeds the system. This is why controversial posts, sensational headlines, and divisive topics tend to dominate our digital spaces. It's not a matter of intent but design; algorithms are not inherently malevolent, but their optimization for engagement can lead to unintended consequences. The prioritization of attention above all else creates an environment where the most provocative content thrives, contributing to echo chambers and polarized discourse. This dynamic is especially troubling because it operates invisibly, subtly nudging users toward certain behaviors or beliefs without their conscious awareness.

Despite their sophistication, algorithms are not infallible. They reflect the biases and priorities of the systems that create them. When the primary goal is engagement, considerations like truthfulness, diversity, and well-being often take a backseat. The result is a digital landscape where the boundaries between entertainment, information, and manipulation blur. Users may feel as though they are making free choices about the content they consume, but these choices are often heavily influenced, if not outright dictated, by algorithmic design. This raises important questions about autonomy and agency in the digital age. Are we truly in control of our online experiences, or are we unwitting participants in a game where the rules are set by entities we do not see and cannot influence?

The allure of algorithms lies in their promise of efficiency and personalization, yet this promise comes at a cost. By prioritizing what keeps us engaged over what challenges or educates us, they risk narrowing our horizons and reinforcing our existing preferences. This is not merely a technical issue but a deeply human one, as it touches on how we understand ourselves, our relationships, and our place in the world. The power of algorithms is undeniable, but with power comes responsibility—a responsibility that extends to the companies designing these systems and to the users navigating their influence. Recognizing the role algorithms play in shaping our digital realities is the first step toward reclaiming a measure of control over how we engage with the world around us.

Visibility and Algorithmic Favoritism

Algorithms are not neutral tools; they are designed to prioritize certain voices, perspectives, and content, thereby shaping the digital landscape we navigate daily. At their core, algorithms act as gatekeepers, determining which posts, videos, or news stories rise to prominence and which ones fade into obscurity. This is not simply a matter of technical efficiency; it is a deeply human decision encoded in mathematical formulas, reflecting the priorities and biases of those who design them. The result is an uneven playing field where visibility can be a privilege granted to those who align with the system's predefined metrics of engagement, leaving others struggling for recognition.

Consider the way social media platforms amplify sensational content. Posts that provoke outrage or extreme emotional responses often achieve higher visibility because algorithms interpret such reactions as indicators of user interest. This dynamic skews public discourse, creating echo chambers where polarizing views dominate while more measured voices are drowned out. For example, the spread of misinformation often outpaces corrections, not because it is more valuable, but because it is more engaging. Algorithms, in their pursuit of maximizing interaction, inadvertently reward the controversial over the factual and the divisive over the unifying.

This favoritism extends beyond content to the individuals and groups that produce it. Influencers and creators who master algorithmic trends—be it the use of trending hashtags, posting at optimal times, or tailoring content to platform-specific preferences—gain disproportionate visibility. Meanwhile, those without the resources or knowledge to play by these rules are often left invisible. This systemic bias not only consolidates power among a select few but also perpetuates inequalities, as smaller or marginalized voices struggle to break through the algorithmic noise.

Moreover, the logic of visibility isn't merely passive; it actively reshapes behavior. Creators are incentivized to conform to algorithmic preferences, often at the expense of authenticity or depth. The pressure to produce content that "performs well" rather than content that is meaningful distorts creative expression and narrows the diversity of perspectives. What emerges is a homogenized digital culture, where uniqueness is overshadowed by the relentless pursuit of virality and engagement metrics.

This algorithmic favoritism has profound societal implications. By amplifying some voices and suppressing others, algorithms subtly dictate what we consider important, valuable, or worthy of attention. They influence not just individual experiences but collective understanding, determining which stories are heard and which are forgotten. In this way, the algorithm becomes a silent editor, curating reality in a manner that benefits corporate goals while neglecting the richness and complexity of human expression. It is a stark reminder that in the attention economy, visibility is not a neutral act but a carefully orchestrated transaction with profound ethical consequences.

REWARDING CONSISTENCY

The relentless demand for consistency embedded within algorithmic frameworks rewards a particular kind of digital behavior: constant engagement. In the attention economy, platforms thrive on sustained user activity, and algorithms are programmed to favor those who feed this insatiable demand. This creates a feedback loop where users are not just encouraged but subtly coerced into prioritizing frequency over quality, perpetuating cycles of compulsive content production and consumption. The more you engage, the more the algorithm rewards you, reinforcing a digital ecosystem that prizes consistency above all else.

For content creators, this means adhering to punishing schedules to maintain visibility. Whether it is daily posts on Instagram, regular uploads on YouTube, or continuous tweets, creators who fall behind in this race risk being penalized by algorithms that deprioritize inactive accounts. This system fosters an environment where breaks are costly, and burnout becomes a near inevitability for those trying to stay relevant. The pressure to consistently feed the algorithm can stifle creativity, as creators feel compelled to churn out material that aligns with platform-specific trends rather than pursuing innovative or thoughtful projects.

For users, the dynamics are equally pervasive. Notifications, badges, and streaks are carefully engineered to encourage ongoing interaction, exploiting psychological principles like loss aversion and reward anticipation. Take, for instance, the "streak" feature on apps like Snapchat, where the incentive to maintain daily contact turns casual interactions into an obligation. Such mechanisms are not accidental; they are designed to keep users tethered to platforms, creating habits that are difficult to break. Over time, these features transform the digital experience into a constant, low-level hum of obligation, leaving users feeling both connected and trapped.

The consequences extend beyond individual behavior. The emphasis on consistency shifts the broader culture of the internet, shaping how content is valued and consumed. Quality becomes secondary to quantity; nuanced, thoughtful contributions struggle to compete with the relentless flood of easily digestible material. Algorithms prioritize what is frequent and predictable, marginalizing content that requires time or effort to produce. This preference for instant gratification reshapes public discourse, rewarding sensationalism and superficial engagement over meaningful dialogue and critical reflection.

The reward system for consistency is not merely an operational choice; it is a deliberate strategy that aligns with the financial goals of platforms. By fostering habitual use, companies ensure a steady flow of data and engagement metrics, which can be monetized through advertising and partnerships. This transactional relationship between user activity and platform profitability underscores the darker side of consistency: the erosion of autonomy. Users and creators alike are subtly manipulated into conforming to patterns of behavior that serve corporate interests, often at the expense of their well-being or creative aspirations.

The algorithmic emphasis on consistency reveals the transactional nature of our relationship with technology. While it offers rewards in the form of visibility and engagement, it exacts a significant cost: the commodification of time, attention, and creativity. In this framework, every moment spent online is both a personal sacrifice and a corporate gain, highlighting the need to reconsider how we engage with platforms that prioritize their bottom line over our humanity.

REAL-WORLD REFLECTIONS

In examining how algorithms shape visibility and spread, three case studies illuminate their profound influence: the amplification of political campaigns, the promotion of specific ideologies, and the suppression of dissent. These real-world examples demonstrate the extraordinary power algorithms wield in shaping public discourse, often with far-reaching consequences.

One striking case is the 2016 U.S. presidential election, during which Donald Trump's campaign demonstrated a masterful understanding of Facebook's algorithmic ecosystem. By leveraging data-driven microtargeting, the campaign saturated key voter demographics with tailored ads that aligned with their fears, beliefs, or frustrations. The Facebook algorithm prioritized engagement, meaning emotionally charged content—whether positive or negative—received higher visibility. Trump's campaign thrived in this environment, deploying ads that generated high levels of interaction, often by exploiting divisive issues. Critics argue that this strategy not only benefited from but actively manipulated the algorithm's preference for sensationalism, shaping the narrative in ways that disadvantaged other candidates. Hillary Clinton's campaign, while robust, struggled to adapt to the algorithmically-driven environment in the same way, demonstrating how such systems can skew political competition based on their inherent biases toward certain content dynamics.

Algorithms don't merely amplify campaigns—they also play a critical role in the spread of ideologies, as evidenced by the rise of anti-vaccination movements on social media platforms like YouTube and Facebook. These platforms, designed to prioritize content that keeps users engaged, often promote extreme or controversial views because they spark heated discussions and prolonged attention. In the case of anti-vaccine rhetoric, YouTube's recommendation system was found to repeatedly suggest videos promoting misinformation to users who had watched related content, creating a self-reinforcing echo chamber. This algorithmic behavior significantly contributed to the resurgence of vaccine skepticism, amplifying fringe beliefs into mainstream discourse. Despite efforts by platforms to counteract misinformation, the damage highlights how algorithms, driven by engagement metrics, can inadvertently elevate harmful narratives over credible, science-based information.

Equally significant is the suppression of voices and ideas that run counter to dominant narratives, often influenced by geopolitical considerations. A notable example is the 2019 Hong Kong protests, during which activists relied heavily on social media to organize and disseminate information globally. However, platforms like Facebook and Twitter faced accusations of algorithmically downplaying protest-related content in certain regions, particularly in mainland China, where governmental pressure loomed large. Simultaneously, pro-government narratives and disinformation campaigns gained traction, aided by the same algorithms that suppressed dissenting voices. The result was a stark asymmetry in visibility, where the struggles of protesters were overshadowed by state-sponsored messaging, showcasing how algorithms can be wielded as tools of influence and control.

These case studies underscore the dual-edged nature of algorithmic power. While they can provide unprecedented reach to individuals and movements, they also create vulnerabilities to manipulation, misinformation, and suppression. As political campaigns, ideologies, and governments continue to adapt their strategies to exploit these systems, the ethical questions surrounding their design and deployment grow ever more urgent. The need for transparency and accountability in algorithmic processes is not just a technical concern—it is a matter of safeguarding democratic values and ensuring equitable access to the digital public sphere.

THE ETHICAL IMPLICATIONS OF ADDICTIVE ALGORITHMS

The ethical implications of addictive algorithms extend far beyond the individual user, permeating the societal fabric in ways that demand urgent reflection. These algorithms, meticulously engineered to optimize engagement, raise fundamental questions about the responsibility of technology companies in shaping human behavior. By exploiting psychological vulnerabilities for profit, these systems blur the line between innovation and manipulation, leaving individuals and communities to grapple with the long-term consequences of their pervasive influence.

At the heart of the ethical dilemma is the deliberate exploitation of human psychology, particularly through mechanisms like intermittent reinforcement and the fear of missing out. As previously discussed, these strategies tap into deep-seated cognitive biases, encouraging compulsive behaviors that prioritize algorithmic profitability over user well-being. The question arises: where should the boundary lie between designing for engagement and respecting the autonomy of users? The addictive nature of these platforms often results in individuals sacrificing time, mental health, and even relationships, a trade-off that is seldom explicit in the terms of service agreements they unwittingly accept.

Moreover, algorithms are not neutral. As seen in their role in amplifying political campaigns or spreading ideologies, they actively shape societal narratives. This power to determine visibility—who is heard and who is not—carries profound ethical weight. For instance, when algorithms favor engagement over truth, they may amplify polarizing or extreme content, exacerbating societal divisions and undermining democratic discourse. The unintended consequence is a digital landscape where misinformation thrives, and nuanced, factual discussions struggle for prominence. Such an environment not only misinforms but also erodes trust in institutions and between individuals.

The structural design of algorithms also raises concerns about inequity. As demonstrated by the Hong Kong protests, these systems can be influenced by geopolitical forces, effectively silencing marginalized voices while amplifying state-sponsored narratives. This asymmetry in visibility reflects broader ethical challenges in global technology governance, where the interests of profit-driven corporations and authoritarian regimes often outweigh the rights of individual users. The suppression of dissenting voices, whether through algorithmic oversight or intentional design, highlights the need for accountability mechanisms that ensure these systems uphold principles of fairness and justice.

The societal cost of addictive algorithms extends to their role in fostering an unsustainable relationship with technology. By prioritizing constant engagement, they contribute to a culture of distraction and cognitive overload, undermining the very capacities that define human agency: focus, critical thinking, and the ability to engage meaningfully with others. The ripple effects are felt not just in individuals' lives but also in broader societal challenges, from declining productivity to the erosion of collective action on pressing global issues. In this sense, the ethical implications are not merely about individual harm but about the systemic risks these technologies pose to social cohesion and progress.

These considerations demand a reevaluation of the ethical frameworks guiding algorithmic design. While innovation and profitability are legitimate goals, they cannot come at the expense of human dignity and autonomy. The challenge lies in balancing the capabilities of algorithms with the ethical imperative to protect individuals and society from their harmful effects. This requires not only corporate responsibility but also robust regulatory oversight and a collective commitment to designing technologies that prioritize humanity over profit.

Exploiting Human Vulnerabilities

The modern attention economy thrives on its ability to exploit deeply ingrained psychological biases, turning human vulnerabilities into mechanisms for profit. These biases, far from being random quirks of human behavior, are rooted in evolutionary and neurological adaptations that once served to enhance survival. In today's world, however, they are weaponized to keep us engaged with technology, often at the expense of our cognitive and emotional well-being. Consider the momentary thrill of a notification or the irresistible urge to refresh a social media feed. These everyday experiences are not incidental; they are the result of deliberate design choices informed by a profound understanding of human psychology.

This manipulation begins with our brain's natural inclination toward novelty, an evolutionary adaptation that ensured attentiveness to changes in our environment. Novel stimuli, signaling potential opportunities or threats, activate the brain's reward system, releasing dopamine and fostering a sense of curiosity and excitement. In the digital age, the novelty effect is amplified by endless streams of updates, notifications, and algorithmically curated content. Social media platforms, streaming services, and even news sites compete relentlessly to deliver the "newest" thing, exploiting this ancient bias to monopolize our attention. Each alert, each refreshed feed taps into this hardwired preference, creating a cycle of constant distraction that leaves us craving more.

Equally potent is the fear of missing out, a bias deeply rooted in our social evolution. Human survival historically depended on inclusion within groups, making exclusion a significant threat. Today, this primal fear manifests as FOMO, a pervasive anxiety that others might be experiencing something valuable or enjoyable without us. Digital platforms exacerbate this fear by curating idealized versions of reality, showing us only the highlights of others' lives while subtly reminding us of our own perceived inadequacies. The constant stream of updates ensures that users feel compelled to stay connected, lest they miss an important opportunity or moment of social validation.

Intermittent reinforcement represents perhaps the most insidious mechanism driving our attachment to digital devices. Drawing from the principles of operant conditioning, this phenomenon occurs when rewards are delivered unpredictably, creating a powerful association between behavior and reward. Early experiments with animals showed that uncertain rewards generated more persistent and compulsive behavior than predictable ones. In the digital realm, features such as variable "likes," unpredictable notifications, and surprise viral content mirror this dynamic. These unpredictable rewards trigger dopamine surges, encouraging users to engage compulsively, often without realizing they are caught in a loop designed to exploit this vulnerability.

These biases do not operate in isolation. They interact and reinforce one another, creating a complex feedback loop that magnifies their effects. A notification, for instance, might initially draw attention through its novelty. The content it reveals could then trigger FOMO, compelling the user to engage further. Finally, the unpredictability of subsequent rewards ensures repeated engagement, forming a cycle that is as self-perpetuating as it is difficult to break. This interplay highlights the evolutionary mismatch between our cognitive architecture and the demands of the digital age. While these biases once served adaptive purposes, they are now exploited in ways that undermine our autonomy and well-being.

Understanding these mechanisms is not merely an academic exercise; it is essential for recognizing how they shape our behaviors and perceptions. The deliberate exploitation of human vulnerabilities by technology companies raises significant ethical questions about the boundaries of persuasion and manipulation. Are these platforms simply meeting our innate preferences, or are they pushing us into states of dependency for profit? The answer lies in critically examining these biases and their role in fostering cognitive overload, setting the stage for a broader discussion about reclaiming agency in the attention economy.

THE NOVELTY EFFECT: THE PULL OF THE NEW

Human beings are inherently drawn to novelty, a tendency deeply rooted in our evolutionary history. In ancient environments, paying attention to new stimuli often meant the difference between survival and peril. The appearance of something unfamiliar—a sound in the underbrush, a sudden change in the landscape—signaled potential danger or opportunity, demanding immediate focus. This bias toward novelty, designed to ensure survival, has been co-opted in the modern era by systems engineered to captivate and hold our attention. Nowhere is this more evident than in the digital platforms that dominate our daily lives.

The brain's reward system plays a central role in the allure of novelty. Encounters with new stimuli activate the dopaminergic pathways, releasing a rush of pleasure and reinforcing the behavior that led to the discovery. Unlike predictable rewards, which quickly lose their appeal, novel stimuli sustain interest, stimulating curiosity and engagement. This neurological mechanism explains why an unexpected notification or a fresh piece of content feels irresistible. Social media platforms, streaming services, and news outlets exploit this response by delivering a continuous stream of updates, each designed to feel unique and important. The mere possibility of encountering something new and exciting keeps users scrolling, clicking, and refreshing, often for hours.

Digital design amplifies the novelty effect by removing barriers to access and embedding it within the very structure of online interactions. Infinite scrolling, for instance, ensures that there is always more content waiting just below the screen's edge, creating an illusion of endless possibilities. Algorithmic curation further heightens the effect by personalizing content, making every new post, video, or recommendation feel uniquely tailored to the individual. This personalization blurs the line between novelty and relevance, making it even harder to resist. Platforms continually adapt, learning from user behavior to deliver ever more engaging—and novel—experiences.

The consequences of this constant bombardment are far-reaching. While the novelty effect provides short-term gratification, its long-term impact on cognitive functioning is less benign. A relentless focus on newness fragments attention, eroding the capacity for sustained concentration and deep thinking. Tasks requiring persistence or focus become increasingly difficult as the brain grows accustomed to the rapid, dopamine-driven rewards of novel stimuli. The result is a state of perpetual distraction, where the craving for the next new thing supersedes the ability to engage meaningfully with the present.

Moreover, the saturation of novelty in the digital space leads to a paradoxical phenomenon: the diminishing returns of novelty itself. As platforms escalate their efforts to capture attention, users become desensitized, requiring even more sensational or provocative content to elicit the same response. This escalation creates a feedback loop, pushing platforms toward ever more aggressive tactics and leaving users in a state of overstimulation. The quest for novelty, once an adaptive trait, becomes a source of cognitive strain and emotional exhaustion.

Understanding the novelty effect is crucial for reclaiming agency in an environment designed to exploit it. By recognizing how platforms leverage this bias, individuals can begin to question their own behaviors and choices. Are we engaging with digital content out of genuine interest, or are we simply responding to the lure of the new? This awareness is the first step toward breaking free from the cycle of distraction, enabling a more intentional and balanced relationship with technology.

THE ANXIETY OF EXCLUSION

The fear of exclusion, a psychological vulnerability deeply ingrained in human nature, exerts a powerful influence on our behaviors in the digital age. Historically, belonging to a group was not merely advantageous but essential for survival. Exclusion often meant isolation, vulnerability, and a diminished chance of thriving. This evolutionary imperative has given rise to an acute sensitivity to social belonging and the fear of being left out—an anxiety now masterfully exploited by the attention economy.

In the context of digital platforms, the fear of missing out (FOMO) represents a modern iteration of this primal anxiety. Social media, in particular, thrives on fostering a sense of perpetual connectedness while simultaneously highlighting what others are doing, achieving, or experiencing in real time. The carefully curated feeds of vacations, celebrations, and milestones are designed not only to share but also to provoke. The algorithms prioritize content that evokes strong emotional reactions, and few emotions are as potent as the unease that comes from feeling left behind. As users scroll through the endless highlights of others' lives, they are subtly reminded of the experiences they are not part of, triggering a cycle of comparison, envy, and compulsive engagement.

Notifications amplify this anxiety by creating a constant state of anticipation. A missed message, an unacknowledged event, or even a delay in checking the latest updates can lead to a heightened sense of exclusion. Platforms craft these interruptions with precision, ensuring they appear urgent even when they are trivial. The red badge, the ping of an alert, and the promise of something new on the screen tap directly into our social anxieties, compelling us to stay tethered to the digital world. Every interaction is framed as a potential moment of connection—or exclusion—making disengagement feel like a risk.

The consequences of this anxiety extend beyond individual behaviors, shaping broader social dynamics and mental health outcomes. The relentless exposure to others' lives through a lens of selective idealism cultivates a distorted perception of reality, where one's own experiences seem inadequate or incomplete. This comparison not only fuels discontent but also diminishes genuine self-worth, as achievements and relationships are measured against a curated and often unattainable standard. The emotional toll of this dynamic is profound, contributing to increased rates of anxiety, depression, and social withdrawal, even as individuals become more digitally connected than ever.

Ironically, the fear of exclusion often results in behaviors that perpetuate exclusion itself. The compulsive need to document and share creates a performative culture, where authenticity is sacrificed for the appearance of participation and relevance. This cycle reinforces the very dynamics it seeks to escape, as individuals strive to prove their inclusion in the narrative while deepening their dependence on the platforms that drive the anxiety.

To address the anxiety of exclusion, one must first recognize its engineered nature. The platforms that profit from this fear do so intentionally, leveraging human vulnerabilities to maximize engagement. Building awareness of this manipulation allows individuals to reclaim agency, questioning the value and purpose of their digital interactions. True connection and fulfillment are not found in the relentless pursuit of belonging as defined by social media but in cultivating meaningful, reciprocal relationships beyond the screen. By reframing exclusion not as a threat but as an opportunity for reflection and autonomy, we can begin to dismantle the structures that exploit our fears and rediscover a more authentic sense of belonging.

THE SLOT MACHINE EFFECT

The slot machine, an iconic symbol of chance and reward, serves as an apt metaphor for one of the most pervasive mechanisms driving digital engagement: intermittent reinforcement. Rooted in behavioral psychology, this principle refers to the unpredictable delivery of rewards, a system that proves more compelling than consistent or predictable gratification. It taps into the human brain's deep-seated drive to seek patterns and rewards, creating a loop of anticipation and satisfaction that is nearly impossible to resist. The architects of the digital world have harnessed this effect with precision, designing platforms that keep users endlessly engaged.

Intermittent reinforcement operates on the fundamental unpredictability of outcomes. In a traditional slot machine, the pull of the lever might yield a jackpot, a small win, or nothing at all. It is this uncertainty that keeps players returning, as the next attempt could always be "the one." Similarly, digital platforms—from social media feeds to email notifications—are built on a comparable system of reward variability. Scrolling through a feed may deliver a mix of mundane updates, emotionally charged posts, or viral content, creating a sense of random discovery that mirrors the allure of the slot machine.

The neurological basis of this effect lies in the brain's dopaminergic system. Dopamine, often associated with pleasure, is more accurately understood as a chemical of anticipation and motivation. The unpredictable nature of intermittent reinforcement maximizes dopamine release, as the brain remains in a heightened state of expectancy, constantly seeking the next reward. This mechanism is why users feel compelled to refresh their social media feeds, open yet another app, or check their notifications—the promise of something gratifying, though uncertain, keeps them locked in a cycle of engagement.

Infinite scrolling, a hallmark feature of many platforms, exemplifies the slot machine effect. The endless stream of content removes natural stopping points, making it easy for users to lose track of time and continue seeking the next hit of novelty or relevance. The algorithmic curation of this content ensures that occasional rewards—a striking image, an intriguing post, or a particularly engaging video—are interspersed unpredictably among less engaging material. Each "win" reinforces the behavior, ensuring users remain hooked.

Notifications and likes also play into this system, delivering small but variable bursts of social validation. A post might garner dozens of reactions or just a few; a message might bring exciting news or a mundane inquiry. This uncertainty fuels compulsive checking, as users hope for the dopamine rush that comes with a positive outcome. Even when the results are disappointing, the potential for future rewards keeps the cycle alive.

The impact of the slot machine effect extends far beyond individual habits, shaping the broader cultural landscape in profound ways. It encourages a fragmented attention span, as users flit between platforms and devices in search of their next digital reward. Over time, this erodes the capacity for sustained focus, deep work, and meaningful engagement. Moreover, it fosters dependency, as the brain begins to crave the dopamine-driven highs of digital interaction, making it increasingly difficult to disengage.

Recognizing the parallels between digital platforms and slot machines is a crucial step toward reclaiming autonomy. Awareness of how intermittent reinforcement manipulates behavior allows individuals to critically evaluate their interactions with technology. Strategies such as setting time limits, creating intentional stopping points, and prioritizing offline activities can help disrupt the cycle. Ultimately, the key lies in understanding that the perceived rewards of digital engagement are carefully engineered to serve the interests of platforms, not users. By reclaiming control over where and how attention is directed, individuals can break free from the pull of the slot machine effect and rediscover the depth and richness of experiences beyond the screen.

INTERACTIONS AND FEEDBACK LOOPS

Human interactions, especially in digital spaces, are increasingly mediated by feedback loops that amplify engagement while subtly shaping behavior. These loops, often rooted in the mechanics of reinforcement and reciprocity, form the backbone of modern online platforms, creating a cycle in which users not only consume content but also contribute to the system's self-sustaining design. By leveraging psychological principles, these interactions create an environment where attention is not merely captured but continuously cultivated.

At the core of these feedback loops is the interplay between user actions and algorithmic responses. When an individual likes a post, comments on a thread, or shares content, their behavior feeds into algorithms designed to learn and adapt. The system responds by presenting tailored recommendations, targeted ads, or curated content streams, creating the illusion of personalization while reinforcing patterns of engagement. Each interaction refines the algorithm's understanding of the user, making subsequent suggestions more relevant, and thus more compelling, further deepening the cycle.

The reciprocity inherent in social interactions also plays a pivotal role in these loops. Social platforms capitalize on the human need for validation and connection by embedding mechanisms that reward users for their participation. Notifications about likes, shares, or responses tap into the desire for acknowledgment, encouraging users to return to the platform to reciprocate or engage further. These seemingly minor acts of validation can trigger profound emotional responses, from satisfaction to anxiety, depending on the feedback received—or withheld. Over time, users may find themselves driven less by intrinsic motivation and more by the pursuit of external validation, subtly altering the nature of their engagement.

Another critical aspect of these feedback loops is their collective impact on group behavior. Social media platforms, for instance, often amplify content that provokes strong emotional reactions, such as outrage, joy, or fear. Algorithms prioritize these high-engagement posts, creating echo chambers where users are repeatedly exposed to content that reinforces their existing beliefs and biases. The feedback loop extends beyond individual interactions, shaping communal discourse and perpetuating cycles of polarization or conformity within digital communities.

These interactions are further reinforced by the gamification of user experiences. Features such as streaks, badges, and progress bars exploit the brain's reward systems, making participation feel like a game where users are compelled to achieve, maintain, or surpass benchmarks. This not only incentivizes frequent engagement but also fosters a sense of competition or comparison among users, deepening their investment in the platform. The gamified elements, while seemingly innocuous, subtly shift focus from meaningful engagement to metrics-driven interaction, often at the expense of authenticity.

The compounding nature of these feedback loops has significant implications for cognitive and emotional well-being. As interactions become increasingly mediated by algorithmic designs, users may find their sense of agency diminished. Rather than engaging intentionally, many find themselves reacting to stimuli orchestrated by platforms, leading to patterns of compulsive use. This can erode attention spans, increase stress, and foster a dependency on external validation for self-worth.

To counteract the effects of these feedback loops, it is crucial to cultivate awareness of how they function and their impact on behavior. Understanding the mechanics behind algorithmic curation, social validation, and gamification can help individuals recognize when their interactions are being driven by design rather than deliberate choice. Strategies such as limiting notifications, practicing intentional consumption, and prioritizing real-world connections can disrupt the loops, allowing for a more autonomous and authentic relationship with technology. By reclaiming the power to shape interactions, individuals can move beyond the cycle of algorithmic manipulation and toward a more mindful and purposeful engagement with digital spaces.

Ethical Reflections

The ethical dimensions of exploiting human psychological vulnerabilities in the design of digital platforms present a profound challenge. At the foundation lies a tension between innovation and integrity: the drive to create engaging, profitable technologies often conflicts with the responsibility to protect users from harm. This conflict is especially salient in the context of behavioral manipulation, where platforms not only anticipate user tendencies but actively shape them, raising fundamental questions about autonomy, consent, and accountability.

A central ethical concern is the asymmetry of power and knowledge between platforms and their users. Companies possess vast amounts of data about individual behaviors, preferences, and weaknesses, enabling them to craft experiences that maximize engagement. Users, on the other hand, often lack both the awareness of these tactics and the resources to resist them. This imbalance undermines informed consent, as individuals may not fully grasp the extent to which their interactions are shaped by algorithms designed to exploit cognitive biases. When users are unaware of the mechanics driving their engagement, their capacity for free choice is diminished, eroding the foundation of ethical interaction.

The commodification of attention also raises significant moral questions. In this paradigm, human focus becomes a resource to be extracted, quantified, and sold. This commodification reduces individuals to economic units, valued not for their well-being but for their ability to generate revenue. Such a reductionist view neglects the broader human experience, ignoring the cognitive and emotional toll of persistent engagement. As users are drawn into cycles of compulsive behavior, the long-term consequences—ranging from diminished mental health to impaired relationships—are externalized, borne by individuals and society rather than the corporations profiting from their attention.

Another ethical issue stems from the societal impacts of these platforms. The amplification of divisive content, the spread of misinformation, and the entrenchment of echo chambers are not incidental but are byproducts of systems optimized for engagement. By prioritizing content that elicits strong emotional responses, platforms inadvertently (or perhaps knowingly) contribute to polarization and social fragmentation. The question then arises: should platforms be held accountable for the societal harm they facilitate, even if such outcomes were not their explicit intent? Ethical design demands that companies take responsibility not only for user-level consequences but also for the broader societal ripple effects of their technologies.

The targeting of vulnerable populations further complicates the ethical landscape. Children, for example, are particularly susceptible to manipulation, lacking the cognitive maturity to recognize or resist exploitative tactics. Similarly, individuals struggling with addiction, loneliness, or mental health challenges may find themselves disproportionately affected by systems designed to capitalize on emotional needs. The exploitation of such vulnerabilities crosses an ethical line, suggesting a need for heightened protections and regulations to safeguard these groups.

Proponents of the status quo often argue that users bear some responsibility for their engagement, citing the availability of tools to manage screen time or customize notifications. However, this perspective overlooks the extent to which platforms are engineered to override self-regulation. The burden of ethical responsibility cannot rest solely on users when the systems themselves are designed to exploit human limitations. True ethical accountability requires that companies acknowledge their role in creating environments that prioritize profit over well-being.

In reflecting on these ethical dilemmas, the path forward becomes clear: a reimagining of technology that places human dignity at its center. This involves designing systems that respect autonomy, prioritize transparency, and mitigate harm. Ethical tech design is not merely an aspirational goal but a necessary shift, requiring collaboration between technologists, policymakers, and ethicists. By fostering a culture of accountability and embedding ethical considerations into the fabric of innovation, we can move toward a digital future that empowers rather than exploits.

The ethical stakes are high, but the potential for change is equally profound. As we confront the challenges posed by cognitive exploitation, we are presented with an opportunity to rethink our relationship with technology and reaffirm the values that guide its development. In doing so, we not only protect individual well-being but also strengthen the societal fabric that binds us together.

Awareness as the First Step

Awareness marks the critical starting point in addressing the pervasive grip of cognitive exploitation. Before change can occur, individuals must first understand the mechanisms that manipulate their behavior, the systems that perpetuate these dynamics, and the impact on their autonomy and well-being. Without this foundational understanding, attempts to mitigate the effects of attention-engineered platforms risk being superficial, addressing symptoms while leaving the underlying structures intact. Awareness, then, is not merely a passive realization but an active process of interrogation and critical reflection, empowering individuals to reclaim agency over their attention.

A key barrier to awareness lies in the invisibility of the forces at play. Behavioral manipulation often operates below the threshold of conscious perception, leveraging automatic processes and subconscious biases. Users may find themselves compelled to scroll, click, or engage without fully understanding why. This opacity is no accident but a deliberate design choice. Notifications, infinite scrolling, and algorithmically curated feeds are presented as benign conveniences, obscuring the intentionality behind their addictive qualities. Recognizing these tactics requires a shift in perspective, where users learn to see their interactions not as organic but as the product of calculated design.

Developing this awareness involves more than understanding individual tactics; it also requires grappling with the broader systemic context. Attention-driven platforms exist within a larger ecosystem where data is harvested, commodified, and leveraged for profit. The interplay between personal behavior and corporate objectives is central to the attention economy, and recognizing this dynamic can help users move beyond self-blame. Cognitive overload is not a failure of personal discipline but a predictable outcome of systems engineered to exploit human vulnerabilities. Awareness thus reframes the problem, shifting the narrative from individual shortcomings to structural inequities.

One of the most effective ways to cultivate awareness is through education, both formal and informal. Digital literacy programs that go beyond basic technical skills to address the psychological and sociological dimensions of technology use can play a transformative role. These programs should aim to demystify the design principles underlying digital platforms, equipping users with the tools to identify manipulative features. Education also extends to fostering critical thinking, encouraging users to question their behaviors and the incentives driving platform design. When individuals understand how and why their attention is commodified, they are better positioned to resist manipulation.

Awareness, however, must also be collective. While individual understanding is vital, the scale of the issue demands a societal response. Conversations around cognitive exploitation must enter the public discourse, challenging the normalization of attention engineering. This includes pushing for transparency from technology companies, advocating for regulatory oversight, and supporting initiatives that prioritize ethical design. Collective awareness amplifies individual efforts, creating a cultural environment that values intentionality and mindfulness over passive consumption.

Yet awareness is not an endpoint; it is a catalyst for action. Understanding the mechanisms of manipulation opens the door to behavioral change and systemic advocacy. On an individual level, this might involve setting boundaries around technology use, adopting tools to mitigate distractions, or prioritizing activities that foster deep focus. On a broader scale, it means holding platforms accountable, demanding ethical innovation, and supporting movements that aim to reshape the digital landscape. Awareness, when coupled with action, becomes a powerful force for reclaiming autonomy in the attention economy.

In fostering awareness, the ultimate goal is to create a culture where intentionality prevails over impulsivity. By shining a light on the hidden forces that shape our behaviors, we empower individuals to make choices aligned with their values and aspirations. This shift not only enhances personal well-being but also lays the groundwork for a more equitable and humane digital future. Awareness, then, is not just the first step but the foundation upon which meaningful change is built.

ENGINEERED ADDICTION

The mechanisms of notifications and infinite scrolling are not incidental byproducts of technological progress but are deliberately engineered to captivate and sustain user engagement. These features, core to the business models of platforms thriving in the attention economy, embody what can be described as engineered addiction. Their design prioritizes metrics such as time spent, click-through rates, and data collection over the autonomy and well-being of users. This is not a mere alignment of convenience with technological capability but a calculated strategy grounded in behavioral science and neuropsychology. Notifications and infinite scrolling are carefully constructed to exploit fundamental vulnerabilities in human attention and reward processing systems, ensuring that disengagement feels both unnatural and difficult.

Notifications disrupt the natural rhythm of cognitive processes, acting as external triggers that demand immediate attention. Each alert is a call to action, a momentary command that taps into the brain's urgency pathways. They are designed to be unpredictable, delivering messages, updates, or interactions at irregular intervals, ensuring that the user remains in a constant state of anticipation. This unpredictability mirrors the mechanisms of variable reinforcement schedules, where rewards are given at irregular intervals, creating a compulsion to check for updates. Over time, this anticipation becomes ingrained, not as a deliberate act but as a reflexive response. Similarly, infinite scrolling eliminates natural stopping points, replacing the traditional concept of "finishing" with a perpetual stream of content. This seamless continuity removes cues for disengagement, immersing the user in a flow state that distorts their perception of time and diminishes conscious decision-making about when to stop.

These features work synergistically, creating a feedback loop where the interruption caused by notifications leads the user back to the infinite scroll. The alert functions as a lure, a gateway to the continuous stream of information designed to hold attention indefinitely. Together, these mechanisms ensure that attention is not merely captured but retained, transformed into a resource extracted for profit. The engineered addiction they foster is subtle but pervasive, embedding itself in the daily routines of users and reshaping their interactions with technology. By capitalizing on the vulnerabilities inherent in human cognition, these tools exemplify the meticulous design of the attention economy, where the primary product is not the content consumed but the user's focus itself.

PSYCHOLOGICAL EXPLOITATION OF ATTENTIONAL BIASES

The psychological exploitation of attentional biases through features like notifications and infinite scrolling is a testament to the deliberate manipulation of human cognitive tendencies. These biases, deeply embedded in our evolutionary and psychological makeup, are neither incidental nor benign in the design of digital platforms. They are systematically targeted to maximize engagement, creating a cycle of compulsive behavior that serves the economic imperatives of the attention economy. Central to this exploitation is the way such features leverage salience, novelty, and immediacy—traits that our attentional systems are inherently primed to prioritize.

Notifications capitalize on the brain's tendency to ascribe significance to immediate stimuli. The sound, vibration, or visual cue of an incoming alert acts as a salient signal that overrides ongoing tasks, activating the brain's orienting response. This response, which evolved to detect and respond to potential threats or opportunities, is exploited in the modern context to ensure that attention is redirected toward the digital platform. Even when notifications are devoid of urgency or substance, their mere presence exploits this attentional bias, compelling users to disengage from their current focus and redirect cognitive resources toward investigating the alert.

Infinite scrolling, on the other hand, manipulates the brain's propensity for seeking novelty and reward. By removing natural stopping cues and presenting an endless stream of content, this design ensures that users are continuously exposed to stimuli that trigger reward pathways. Each scroll becomes an opportunity to encounter something new, activating the dopaminergic system and creating a reinforcing loop that is difficult to interrupt. This dynamic plays into the attentional bias toward novelty, a mechanism that evolved to help humans learn and adapt but is now co-opted to keep them tethered to the platform.

Together, these features exploit the brain's susceptibility to attentional hijacking, amplifying the effects through their combination. Notifications function as triggers, interrupting focus and prompting a return to the platform, while infinite scrolling ensures prolonged engagement by keeping the user in a state of continuous exploration. This interplay not only reinforces the habitual use of digital platforms but also creates a psychological environment where disengagement feels counterintuitive. By aligning their design with the cognitive architecture of attentional biases, these tools ensure that focus is not only captured but held hostage, underscoring the deeply manipulative nature of the attention economy.

BEHAVIORAL DESIGN AND INTERACTION PATTERNS

Behavioral design and interaction patterns are central to the effectiveness of notifications and infinite scrolling, carefully crafted to exploit subconscious processes that govern decision-making and behavior. These patterns are not accidental but the result of deliberate experimentation aimed at maximizing user engagement. By embedding principles of behavioral psychology into interface design, digital platforms manipulate actions in subtle yet powerful ways, ensuring that users remain locked in cycles of interaction that benefit the platforms' economic goals.

At the core of behavioral design lies the principle of cue-action-reward loops, a psychological framework that guides much of human behavior. Notifications act as cues, triggering an automatic response that compels users to interact with the platform. These cues are designed to be irresistibly intrusive—vibrations, sounds, and visual markers are calibrated to demand attention immediately, overriding conscious decision-making. Importantly, the unpredictability of these cues amplifies their effectiveness. Users are conditioned to expect variability in the type or importance of notifications, which keeps them engaged in a state of anticipatory alertness. This mirrors the psychological mechanics of variable reward systems, deeply ingrained in behaviors associated with gambling and addiction.

Infinite scrolling complements these cue-reward dynamics by fostering a seamless and frictionless user experience. The absence of natural stopping points removes a critical moment for self-regulation, making it harder for users to reflect on their usage patterns or disengage. Each interaction with the scroll is a micro-decision, yet the design masks these decisions, allowing the user to continue consuming content passively. The algorithmic personalization of content further deepens this cycle by tailoring material to individual preferences and behaviors. This personalization ensures that the content encountered is not only engaging but increasingly difficult to resist, reinforcing patterns of compulsive consumption.

Another critical component of interaction patterns is the intentional minimization of effort required to engage with the platform. Features like autoplay, endless feeds, and simplified input mechanisms eliminate barriers to continued use. These design choices align with the human preference for cognitive ease, reducing the mental load associated with decision-making and increasing the likelihood of prolonged engagement. By removing friction, platforms engineer interactions that feel intuitive and natural, further embedding habitual use.

The interplay between behavioral design and interaction patterns reveals a sophisticated strategy to exploit the vulnerabilities of human psychology. These mechanisms ensure that users not only engage with platforms but do so in a way that becomes automatic, habitual, and deeply ingrained. While appearing to enhance convenience and user experience, these patterns are, in reality, tools of manipulation that prioritize the monetization of attention over the well-being of the individual.

Socio-Cultural Amplification

The socio-cultural context in which notifications and infinite scrolling operate serves as a powerful amplifier of their effectiveness, embedding these design mechanisms into the fabric of modern life. In a hyperconnected world, where digital interactions often supplant or mediate face-to-face relationships, these tools gain traction not just as technical features but as cultural norms. Their influence extends beyond individual psychology, shaping collective behaviors, societal expectations, and even the architecture of daily life.

Notifications have transformed from optional alerts into essential threads in the social fabric. The act of receiving a notification often carries an implicit social expectation of responsiveness, creating a sense of urgency that transcends the digital sphere. This urgency is reinforced by a culture that prizes immediacy—whether in professional communication, social interactions, or access to news. Platforms capitalize on this expectation by framing notifications as indispensable to staying connected, informed, and relevant. This cultural framing makes it increasingly difficult for individuals to ignore or disengage, as doing so risks perceived social isolation or professional disadvantage.

Infinite scrolling, too, derives strength from its integration into cultural patterns of consumption. The continuous flow of content mirrors the ethos of abundance that permeates modern life, where more is always seen as better. This aligns with societal values that reward constant productivity and information gathering, creating a feedback loop in which users feel compelled to consume endlessly to stay informed, entertained, or competitive. The design of infinite scrolling exploits these cultural imperatives, presenting an unbroken stream of material that both satisfies and perpetuates the societal pressure to remain engaged.

Furthermore, these tools thrive on the collective fear of falling behind in an era where digital spaces are the primary arenas for information exchange, activism, and social bonding. Notifications often signal trending topics, viral phenomena, or breaking news, prompting users to participate in or at least witness these shared cultural moments. Infinite scrolling ensures that the user has the means to explore these moments endlessly, weaving individual consumption patterns into a broader cultural narrative. In this way, these mechanisms reinforce each other, creating an ecosystem where constant engagement is not just a personal habit but a cultural expectation.

The socio-cultural amplification of these design features also reshapes broader norms around attention and presence. The ubiquity of notifications and the omnipresence of scrolling diminish the value of sustained focus and deep engagement, redefining what it means to be attentive. This shift affects everything from interpersonal relationships to workplace dynamics, where the constant pull of digital interaction fragments attention and reduces the capacity for meaningful connection or creativity. As these norms take hold, they perpetuate a cycle where the tools designed to command attention become indispensable elements of the socio-cultural landscape, further embedding their influence.

In this way, the effectiveness of notifications and infinite scrolling is magnified by their resonance with societal values and behaviors. Their design taps into deep psychological vulnerabilities, but it is the socio-cultural amplification of these mechanisms that ensures their pervasiveness, shaping not only individual habits but the collective experience of life in the digital age.

Cognitive and Emotional Consequences

The relentless pull of notifications and infinite scrolling extends far beyond their immediate interaction, manifesting in profound cognitive and emotional consequences that reshape how individuals think, feel, and engage with the world. These consequences, while often subtle in the short term, accumulate over time to produce a state of persistent fragmentation and mental exhaustion. The interplay between cognitive strain and emotional turbulence becomes an inescapable byproduct of a digital ecosystem designed to monopolize attention.

Cognitively, the constant influx of notifications fragments thought processes, reducing the capacity for sustained focus and deep work. Each alert acts as a micro-interruption, pulling users out of their current cognitive state and demanding reallocation of attention. This disrupts working memory, as the mind struggles to reorient itself back to the task at hand. Over time, these interruptions erode cognitive efficiency, diminishing the ability to concentrate on complex problems or engage in creative thinking. The phenomenon of "switch cost," wherein mental resources are depleted during transitions between tasks, exacerbates the strain, leaving individuals with less mental energy for intentional, purposeful activities.

Infinite scrolling compounds this cognitive toll by fostering a state of passive consumption. The unending stream of content denies the user natural stopping cues, prolonging engagement well beyond intentional use. This immersion in low-effort, high-stimulus activity reinforces shallow processing, where information is skimmed but not retained or critically analyzed. Over time, this habitual engagement weakens the brain's capacity for higher-order thinking, such as reflection, synthesis, and judgment, as these faculties are underutilized in the endless pursuit of fleeting stimuli.

The emotional consequences are equally significant. Notifications, particularly those tied to social validation, tap into deeply rooted needs for acceptance and belonging. While the immediate response to a notification may be a rush of dopamine-fueled anticipation, the longer-term effect is often heightened anxiety. Users become conditioned to expect constant interaction, leading to a baseline state of hypervigilance. This anticipation of interruptions fosters feelings of unease, even when notifications are absent, as individuals grow accustomed to their omnipresence. Over time, this dynamic can create a feedback loop of emotional dependency, where the absence of notifications feels like a void, compelling users to seek validation through further engagement.

Infinite scrolling similarly affects emotional well-being by promoting feelings of dissatisfaction and overstimulation. The relentless exposure to curated content, whether it be aspirational lifestyles or catastrophic news, creates a skewed perception of reality. Users may oscillate between envy, fear, and despair as they compare their own lives to the idealized or alarming narratives presented in the scroll. Additionally, the sheer volume of information can lead to emotional numbing, where the capacity to respond empathetically or meaningfully is diminished due to overstimulation. This phenomenon, often referred to as "compassion fatigue," highlights how infinite scrolling not only affects the individual but also undermines collective emotional engagement.

Together, these cognitive and emotional consequences create a state of chronic distraction and discontent, where individuals are perpetually occupied but rarely fulfilled. This cycle of fragmentation and overstimulation reflects the deeper cost of a design ethos that prioritizes engagement metrics over human well-being. Over time, the erosion of cognitive and emotional resilience undermines not only individual potential but also the capacity for societal progress, as collective attention becomes increasingly diffuse and disengaged. Recognizing these consequences is essential to understanding the true cost of living in an attention economy, where the commodification of focus comes at the expense of mental and emotional health.

Ethical Dimensions

The ethical dimensions of notifications and infinite scrolling transcend individual experiences, delving into broader questions about responsibility, agency, and the moral obligations of designers and technology companies. At the core of this issue lies the tension between the pursuit of profit and the preservation of human autonomy, a dynamic that raises profound concerns about the societal consequences of prioritizing engagement over well-being. This exploration demands a critical examination of the values embedded in technological design and the power dynamics that govern its deployment.

One central ethical issue is the asymmetry of knowledge and power between users and developers. Designers and companies operate with an intimate understanding of the psychological and neurological mechanisms that drive human behavior, leveraging this knowledge to create systems that are difficult, if not impossible, for users to resist. Notifications, crafted with precision to exploit attentional triggers, and infinite scrolling, engineered to eliminate stopping points, exemplify the use of behavioral insights to nudge individuals into prolonged engagement. While this may be justified as innovation or progress, it raises questions about consent, as users are rarely fully aware of the extent to which their actions are being influenced.

The commodification of attention further complicates these ethical considerations. In the attention economy, user engagement translates directly into revenue, whether through advertising, data collection, or subscription models. This monetization creates a conflict of interest, where optimizing for profit often means compromising user well-being. Ethical dilemmas arise when companies knowingly design features that contribute to cognitive overload, emotional distress, or addictive behaviors. The deliberate erosion of boundaries—between work and leisure, focus and distraction—transforms attention into a currency, traded without adequate safeguards to protect its finite nature.

Moreover, the societal implications of these design choices must be considered. The aggregation of individual distraction contributes to a collective fragmentation of focus, undermining public discourse, civic engagement, and the ability to address complex global challenges. Infinite scrolling and persistent notifications exacerbate the polarization of ideas, as users are steered into echo chambers or inundated with sensationalist content designed to provoke emotional reactions. This erosion of shared attention and critical thought is not merely a side effect but an ethical failing of a system that prioritizes engagement over enlightenment.

These issues also highlight questions about equity and justice. Vulnerable populations, including children, adolescents, and individuals with preexisting mental health conditions, are disproportionately affected by manipulative design practices. The universal accessibility of notifications and infinite scrolling ensures that their impacts are pervasive, yet not all users possess the resources or awareness to mitigate these effects. This disparity raises ethical concerns about the role of technology in exacerbating existing inequalities, rather than serving as a tool for empowerment and inclusion.

Finally, the ethical dimensions of this issue demand accountability. While users bear some responsibility for their choices, the burden cannot rest solely on individuals in a system deliberately stacked against their capacity for self-regulation. Designers, policymakers, and technology leaders must confront their roles in perpetuating harm and take proactive steps to align their practices with principles of human dignity and respect. Transparency in design, user education, and the promotion of alternative business models that do not rely on exploitative engagement are essential to addressing these concerns.

The ethical challenges of notifications and infinite scrolling are not insurmountable, but they require a paradigm shift in how technology is conceived and deployed. Moving from an extractive model to one that prioritizes human flourishing demands a recalibration of values—one that places autonomy, equity, and collective well-being at the center of technological innovation. Recognizing the profound ethical stakes involved in these seemingly mundane features is the first step toward creating a digital environment that respects the complexity and sanctity of human attention.

The Rise of Cognitive Overload

Cognitive overload is a state in which the cognitive demands placed on an individual exceed their available mental resources, resulting in impaired processing, retention, and response capabilities. It occurs when the sheer volume or complexity of information overwhelms the mind's ability to manage, filter, and prioritize effectively. Rooted in the finite capacity of working memory, which serves as the brain's temporary storage system for handling and manipulating information, cognitive overload is not merely a consequence of distraction but a fundamental breakdown in the mind's ability to operate within its natural limits.

To understand cognitive overload, it is essential to contextualize it within the frameworks of cognitive psychology and neuroscience. Cognitive Load Theory, proposed by John Sweller, offers a foundational perspective by categorizing the demands on cognition into three types: intrinsic, extraneous, and germane loads. Intrinsic load reflects the inherent complexity of the information being processed, while extraneous load is created by unnecessary or poorly designed information inputs, such as the clutter of a poorly structured digital interface. Germane load, in contrast, refers to the cognitive effort devoted to integrating and understanding information. Cognitive overload arises when the combined weight of these loads exceeds working memory's limited capacity, leading to inefficiencies and errors in thought processes.

Working memory, as outlined in Baddeley and Hitch's model, is a dynamic system capable of holding a small amount of information in an active state for immediate use. However, it is inherently limited, often constrained to approximately four to seven discrete items at a time. This constraint means that when too much information competes for attention, some of it is inevitably lost or inadequately processed. The result is an impaired ability to retain and synthesize information, which can cascade into long-term memory deficits. Overload disrupts the encoding process, where experiences and information are transformed into durable memory traces, diminishing the likelihood of recall and meaningful understanding over time.

At a neurological level, cognitive overload reflects the limitations of the prefrontal cortex, the region of the brain responsible for executive functions such as attention regulation, planning, and decision-making. This part of the brain operates as the central hub for managing incoming stimuli, but it is highly sensitive to excessive demands. Studies utilizing neuroimaging techniques, such as functional magnetic resonance imaging (fMRI), have revealed that when individuals are exposed to overwhelming amounts of information, the prefrontal cortex becomes hyperactive, attempting to process and prioritize inputs, yet quickly reaches a state of diminished efficiency. The consequence is a breakdown in neural coherence, where critical pathways that facilitate cognitive integration are disrupted.

Cognitive overload is not a new phenomenon; its existence can be traced to human cognition's evolutionary roots, where attention was a survival mechanism honed to detect and respond to immediate environmental threats. In contemporary society, this evolutionary trait is exploited by an environment saturated with information designed to captivate and retain attention. The rise of digital technology, with its incessant notifications, algorithmically curated content, and infinite scrolling mechanisms, has exacerbated the issue. Unlike the manageable stimuli of pre-digital eras, today's information landscape operates at a pace and intensity far beyond what the human brain evolved to process, resulting in a chronic state of overload for many.

The phenomenon of cognitive overload can also be understood through its pervasive effects on emotional and behavioral patterns. While its neurological basis lies in the overstimulation of the prefrontal cortex, the consequences extend into the emotional and physiological domains. Overloaded individuals often experience heightened stress levels, stemming from the brain's continuous engagement with unrelenting cognitive demands. This stress further exacerbates the overload by narrowing attentional focus, creating a feedback loop that impairs overall mental clarity.

Ultimately, cognitive overload represents a convergence of biological limits, psychological mechanisms, and sociocultural conditions. As digital technology increasingly encroaches on every aspect of life, the concept has gained particular relevance, underscoring the tension between the human mind's natural boundaries and the artificially amplified demands of modern environments. Understanding its nuances provides a crucial foundation for addressing its broader implications, not only for individual well-being but for society at large, where collective cognitive resources are similarly strained.

IMPACT ON MEMORY

Cognitive overload exerts profound and multifaceted effects on memory, disrupting processes essential for encoding, storage, and retrieval. Memory operates as a complex, multi-stage system, with each phase vulnerable to the detrimental impacts of excessive cognitive demands. At its core, the relationship between cognitive overload and memory is mediated by the limitations of working memory, which serves as the gateway to deeper cognitive processing and long-term retention. When the volume or complexity of incoming information exceeds the capacity of working memory, it not only impairs immediate comprehension but also disrupts the mechanisms required for transferring information into long-term storage.

Encoding, the initial phase of memory formation, is particularly sensitive to cognitive overload. Encoding requires focused attention and sufficient cognitive resources to transform external stimuli into neural representations. Under conditions of overload, the prefrontal cortex, which coordinates attention and working memory, becomes overburdened. This results in a fragmented or incomplete processing of information, diminishing the quality of encoding. For instance, when multiple streams of information compete for attention—such as during multitasking—only superficial aspects of the stimuli may be registered, leaving the deeper, contextual details unattended. This phenomenon explains why individuals often struggle to recall specifics from situations where they were overwhelmed by information, as the initial encoding was inadequate.

Moreover, cognitive overload disrupts consolidation, the process by which memories are stabilized and integrated into the brain's long-term storage. Consolidation relies heavily on the brain's ability to prioritize and organize information, processes that are typically facilitated during periods of rest or focused reflection. However, in an overstimulated state, the brain's resources are directed toward managing immediate demands, leaving little capacity for the intricate neural activities required for consolidation. Research in neuroscience has demonstrated that constant exposure to stimuli—such as persistent engagement with digital devices—can interfere with the brain's ability to form durable memory traces. This interference is compounded by the reduced quality and quantity of sleep often associated with cognitive overload, as sleep is critical for memory consolidation through mechanisms such as hippocampal replay and synaptic pruning.

The retrieval phase of memory is similarly compromised under cognitive overload. Successful retrieval depends on the brain's ability to access stored information using cues and associations established during encoding. However, when cognitive resources are stretched thin, retrieval pathways can become obstructed. Overload-induced stress and mental fatigue impair the brain's executive functions, which are crucial for organizing and selecting relevant memories. This explains the common experience of "blanking out" during high-pressure situations where cognitive demands are excessive. Additionally, the presence of too much irrelevant or competing information—often referred to as "information clutter"—can obscure the retrieval process, making it difficult to isolate the specific memory needed.

At a neurological level, these disruptions to memory are rooted in the overstimulation of key brain regions involved in memory processing, particularly the hippocampus and the prefrontal cortex. The hippocampus, central to the formation and retrieval of declarative memories, becomes less efficient under conditions of sustained cognitive overload. Chronic exposure to stressors associated with overload—such as incessant digital notifications—can even result in structural changes to the hippocampus, including reductions in volume, as observed in studies of individuals exposed to long-term stress or information saturation. Similarly, the prefrontal cortex, which plays a regulatory role in memory processes, struggles to maintain its integrative functions when cognitive demands surpass its capacity.

Cognitive overload also affects working memory, the temporary storage system integral to the execution of complex tasks. Working memory not only handles the immediate manipulation of information but also acts as a bridge to long-term memory. When overwhelmed, working memory's limited capacity is quickly exhausted, leading to errors in processing and a breakdown in the sequential flow of thought. This creates a cascading effect, where incomplete or poorly processed information is passed into long-term storage, further diminishing the quality and utility of retained memories.

The cumulative impact of cognitive overload on memory is not merely a technical limitation but has significant implications for everyday life. The inability to encode and retrieve information effectively affects decision-making, learning, and interpersonal interactions. In professional contexts, for example, individuals experiencing overload may struggle to retain critical details from meetings or to synthesize information needed for strategic planning. In personal contexts, the erosion of memory quality can hinder the formation of meaningful relationships, as the ability to recall shared experiences or important details diminishes.

Ultimately, cognitive overload represents a direct threat to the integrity of memory systems, undermining both individual and collective capacities to process, store, and utilize information meaningfully. As the modern world continues to demand more from human attention, the erosion of memory quality serves as a stark reminder of the finite nature of cognitive resources and the need to protect and prioritize their optimal use.

IMPACT ON DECISION-MAKING

Cognitive overload significantly impairs decision-making, a process that relies on the brain's ability to analyze information, weigh options, and choose a course of action. Decision-making draws heavily on working memory, executive function, and emotional regulation—systems that are particularly vulnerable to the overstimulation and resource depletion caused by excessive cognitive demands. As the modern environment floods individuals with information and constant stimuli, the capacity for thoughtful, deliberate decision-making is undermined, often leading to impulsive, suboptimal, or delayed choices.

At the core of decision-making lies the brain's capacity to process relevant information while filtering out the irrelevant. Cognitive overload disrupts this balance by saturating working memory, leaving insufficient resources to prioritize or organize inputs effectively. Instead of systematically evaluating options, individuals faced with an overwhelming influx of information often resort to heuristic shortcuts—mental rules of thumb designed to simplify complex decision-making. While these heuristics can be adaptive in low-stakes situations, their reliance under conditions of overload frequently results in cognitive biases, such as overconfidence, anchoring, or reliance on the most immediately available information. For example, in a scenario where a consumer is bombarded with marketing messages for a product, they may rely on a single, salient feature—such as price or brand familiarity—rather than a comprehensive evaluation of the product's overall value.

The stress associated with cognitive overload further compounds its detrimental effects on decision-making. Elevated levels of stress hormones, such as cortisol, impair the functioning of the prefrontal cortex, the region of the brain responsible for rational thought and planning. Under these conditions, individuals are more likely to experience decision paralysis, where the inability to process and organize excessive information leads to inaction. This phenomenon is particularly evident in high-stakes environments, such as healthcare, where medical professionals must make complex, time-sensitive decisions. Research has shown that under cognitive overload, even experienced clinicians may default to habitual practices or oversimplified protocols, potentially overlooking nuanced aspects of patient care.

Cognitive overload also disrupts the integration of emotion and logic, an essential component of effective decision-making. Contrary to traditional views of decision-making as purely rational, neuroscience has demonstrated that emotions play a critical role in guiding choices, particularly under uncertainty. The overstimulation associated with cognitive overload destabilizes the limbic system, which governs emotional responses, while simultaneously diminishing the regulatory control of the prefrontal cortex. This imbalance results in heightened emotional reactivity, such as anxiety or frustration, which can cloud judgment and skew decision-making processes. For instance, an individual overwhelmed by competing work deadlines may prioritize tasks based on perceived urgency rather than actual importance, driven more by an emotional need to alleviate immediate stress than by rational assessment.

In addition, cognitive overload diminishes the capacity for reflective and strategic thinking, which are essential for long-term planning and complex decision-making. The constant bombardment of stimuli fragments attention, preventing the sustained focus needed to engage in deliberative thought. As a result, individuals often default to reactive, short-term decisions that address immediate pressures but fail to consider broader implications. This trend has societal repercussions, particularly in political or environmental contexts, where cognitive overload among the public and policymakers alike can lead to a focus on superficial or immediate issues at the expense of addressing systemic, long-term challenges. The rapid consumption of information in digital spaces—often presented in emotionally charged, bite-sized formats—exacerbates this phenomenon by encouraging shallow engagement with complex issues.

At a neural level, the detrimental effects of cognitive overload on decision-making are linked to the interplay between the prefrontal cortex and the amygdala. The prefrontal cortex, responsible for executive functions such as planning, impulse control, and problem-solving, is particularly susceptible to resource depletion under conditions of overload. As its regulatory capacity diminishes, the amygdala, which processes emotional stimuli, exerts greater influence on behavior. This shift from deliberative to reactive decision-making is evident in scenarios where individuals under cognitive stress make choices driven by fear, anger, or immediate gratification rather than rational deliberation.

Moreover, cognitive overload fosters over-reliance on external cues and automation in decision-making. Faced with overwhelming information, individuals increasingly defer to algorithms, default settings, or the opinions of authority figures to reduce cognitive strain. While this reliance can be efficient in certain contexts, it also raises ethical and practical concerns, particularly when algorithms or external influences are biased or prioritize profit over individual well-being. For instance, consumers inundated with options on e-commerce platforms may rely on algorithmic recommendations, unknowingly perpetuating echo chambers or limiting their exposure to diverse choices.

The cumulative impact of cognitive overload on decision-making is both individual and systemic. On a personal level, it erodes confidence in one's ability to navigate complexity, fostering decision fatigue—a psychological state characterized by diminished energy and impaired judgment following repeated decision-making. On a collective level, the prevalence of suboptimal or reactive decisions contributes to inefficiencies, inequities, and missed opportunities for innovation across industries and institutions.

Addressing the decision-making challenges posed by cognitive overload requires both individual strategies and systemic interventions. On the individual level, cultivating practices such as mindfulness, prioritization, and simplification can help conserve cognitive resources for critical decisions. Systemically, the design of information environments must be reimagined to promote clarity, relevance, and accessibility, mitigating the cognitive burdens imposed by modern technologies. Ultimately, understanding and mitigating the effects of cognitive overload on decision-making is essential not only for personal well-being but also for fostering thoughtful, informed choices in an increasingly complex world.

IMPACT ON EMOTIONAL REGULATION

Cognitive overload profoundly disrupts emotional regulation, the ability to manage and respond to emotional experiences in adaptive and socially acceptable ways. Emotional regulation relies on the intricate interplay between the prefrontal cortex, which governs rational thought and impulse control, and the limbic system, particularly the amygdala, which processes emotional stimuli. Under conditions of cognitive overload, the prefrontal cortex is increasingly taxed, diminishing its regulatory influence and leaving individuals more vulnerable to emotional instability. The result is a heightened sensitivity to stress, impaired coping mechanisms, and a cascade of negative emotional outcomes.

One of the most immediate effects of cognitive overload is an increase in emotional reactivity. When the brain is inundated with information and stimuli, the capacity for thoughtful evaluation of emotional triggers is compromised. This creates a state in which even minor provocations can elicit disproportionate emotional responses, such as frustration, irritability, or anxiety. Studies in neuroscience have shown that cognitive overload weakens the connectivity between the prefrontal cortex and the amygdala, effectively reducing the brain's ability to temper emotional impulses with rational assessment. For example, an individual navigating a crowded inbox while juggling multiple deadlines might react to a routine email with anger or panic, perceiving it as an insurmountable demand rather than a manageable task.

Cognitive overload also interferes with the ability to identify, process, and regulate emotions effectively, a phenomenon known as emotional dysregulation. Under normal circumstances, the brain categorizes and prioritizes emotional inputs, allowing individuals to engage with their feelings constructively. However, the constant barrage of stimuli in the attention economy fragments this process, leading to emotional confusion and overwhelm. This is particularly problematic in environments where emotional clarity is essential, such as conflict resolution or caregiving. For instance, a parent overwhelmed by the demands of balancing work emails and household responsibilities may misinterpret a child's need for attention as defiance, responding with undue anger or dismissal rather than empathy.

Another significant consequence of cognitive overload is the erosion of emotional resilience—the capacity to recover from emotional setbacks and adapt to challenges. Chronic overstimulation activates the body's stress-response system, elevating cortisol levels and creating a state of hyperarousal. Over time, this persistent activation impairs the brain's ability to return to a baseline emotional state, fostering chronic anxiety, mood instability, and even depressive tendencies. Emotional resilience, which depends on the prefrontal cortex's ability to contextualize stressors and foster a sense of perspective, is undermined when cognitive resources are perpetually depleted. This dynamic is particularly evident in professional settings, where workers subjected to high cognitive demands and minimal recovery time report greater emotional exhaustion and burnout.

Moreover, cognitive overload disrupts the social aspects of emotional regulation, impairing the ability to interpret and respond appropriately to the emotions of others. Emotional regulation often occurs in a social context, drawing on cues from interpersonal interactions to modulate one's own emotional states. However, cognitive overload limits the brain's capacity for empathy and attentiveness, reducing the quality of social exchanges. This is particularly detrimental in relationships, where emotional attunement is key to building trust and resolving conflicts. A partner preoccupied with digital distractions, for instance, may fail to notice subtle signs of distress in their significant other, leading to misunderstandings or feelings of neglect.

The role of cognitive overload in fostering emotional numbness—an avoidance strategy that dulls emotional experiences to reduce stress—is another critical area of concern. When cognitive demands exceed the brain's processing capacity, individuals may unconsciously suppress emotional responses as a coping mechanism. While this may provide short-term relief, emotional numbness often comes at the expense of long-term well-being, diminishing the capacity for joy, connection, and meaningful engagement with life. The rise of passive consumption behaviors, such as mindless scrolling on social media, reflects this tendency, as individuals turn to low-effort, emotionally neutral activities to escape the overwhelming demands of the digital world.

From a neurochemical perspective, cognitive overload exacerbates imbalances in the brain's reward and stress systems, further undermining emotional regulation. The overactivation of dopamine pathways, driven by the constant novelty and instant gratification offered by digital technologies, creates a cycle of dependence that diminishes the brain's sensitivity to natural rewards. Simultaneously, the chronic stress induced by cognitive overload disrupts the release of serotonin and oxytocin, neurotransmitters essential for emotional stability and social bonding. These neurochemical shifts contribute to a sense of emotional volatility, loneliness, and disconnection, compounding the psychological toll of cognitive overload.

The cumulative effects of cognitive overload on emotional regulation extend beyond the individual, influencing societal dynamics. Widespread emotional dysregulation, fueled by overstimulation and fragmented attention, fosters polarization, hostility, and a decline in collective emotional intelligence. Online discourse, characterized by reactive and often inflammatory exchanges, illustrates how cognitive overload diminishes the capacity for empathy and constructive dialogue. In extreme cases, this environment can escalate into emotional contagion, where unchecked negative emotions spread rapidly across social networks, amplifying collective stress and division.

To mitigate the impact of cognitive overload on emotional regulation, individuals and systems must prioritize practices that restore cognitive and emotional balance. Mindfulness techniques, such as meditation and deep breathing, can strengthen the prefrontal cortex's regulatory capacities, fostering greater emotional awareness and control. On a broader scale, the design of digital environments must shift from exploiting emotional vulnerabilities to supporting emotional well-being, emphasizing clarity, intentionality, and meaningful engagement. Ultimately, addressing the emotional consequences of cognitive overload is not only essential for personal mental health but also for fostering a more empathetic and emotionally resilient society.

BRIDGING THE HISTORICAL CONTEXT

The phenomenon of cognitive overload, while seemingly unique to the modern digital age, has deep historical roots that reveal its recurrence in the face of transformative technological advancements. Each major leap in information dissemination has disrupted the equilibrium of human attention, forcing society to adapt to new paradigms of cognitive engagement. From the advent of the printing press to the rise of television, these innovations have expanded access to information while simultaneously challenging the brain's capacity to process it. By situating the current attention crisis within this historical context, it becomes evident that while the tools and mediums have evolved, the core struggle between human cognition and information abundance remains consistent.

The introduction of the printing press in the 15th century marked one of the earliest instances of a profound cognitive shift triggered by technological advancement. Prior to its invention, access to information was limited, with manuscripts painstakingly copied by hand and literacy confined to societal elites. The printing press democratized knowledge, enabling the mass production of books and a rapid increase in the dissemination of ideas. While this innovation spurred intellectual growth, it also introduced the concept of information overload for the first time. Renaissance scholars lamented the overwhelming flood of texts, fearing that the sheer volume of information would lead to superficial understanding rather than deep intellectual engagement. The historian Ann Blair, in her work *Too Much to Know*, documents how early modern thinkers grappled with this dilemma, developing tools like indexes and reference guides to manage the growing body of knowledge.

Centuries later, the advent of the telegraph and later the telephone reshaped the temporal dimensions of information exchange. These technologies compressed time and space, allowing messages to traverse vast distances almost instantaneously. While this acceleration of communication facilitated commerce, diplomacy, and personal connection, it also created new cognitive challenges. The telegraph, for example, inundated recipients with fragmented bits of information that required rapid interpretation and response, foreshadowing the fragmented attention patterns seen in today's digital notifications. Similarly, the telephone introduced a culture of immediacy, where the expectation of instant availability began to erode the boundaries between personal focus and external demands.

The 20th century witnessed another major disruption with the rise of broadcast media, particularly radio and television. These mediums revolutionized how information was consumed, shifting from the active engagement of reading to the passive reception of audio-visual content. While radio and television broadened access to entertainment and news, they also intensified competition for attention. Television, in particular, became a central fixture of daily life, saturating viewers with a constant stream of advertisements, sensationalist news, and rapid-fire imagery. Scholars like Neil Postman, in *Amusing Ourselves to Death*, critiqued the medium's impact on public discourse, arguing that its emphasis on brevity and spectacle reduced the capacity for deep reflection and critical analysis. This critique presciently echoes the concerns raised about digital platforms today, where algorithms prioritize viral content over substantive dialogue.

What distinguishes the current era from these historical precedents is the sheer scale, speed, and personalization of cognitive demands. Digital technologies, powered by the internet, smartphones, and artificial intelligence, have created an environment where information is not merely abundant but omnipresent. Unlike the printing press or television, which required deliberate engagement, modern digital tools seamlessly integrate into every facet of daily life. Notifications, social media feeds, and targeted advertisements continually vie for attention, leveraging sophisticated algorithms to predict and exploit individual cognitive patterns. This personalization creates a feedback loop where users are perpetually bombarded with stimuli tailored to their preferences and vulnerabilities, amplifying the intensity of cognitive overload.

Moreover, the democratization of content creation in the digital age has exponentially increased the volume of information. Social media platforms like Twitter (now X) and TikTok enable millions of users to generate and share content in real time, creating a deluge of data that far exceeds the human brain's capacity to process. This phenomenon is further compounded by the 24/7 news cycle, which prioritizes speed over accuracy, inundating audiences with breaking stories, updates, and opinions. Unlike past eras, where information dissemination was largely centralized and curated, the current landscape is characterized by decentralization and constant flux, leaving individuals with the burden of filtering and prioritizing information amidst the chaos.

The transition from episodic to continuous engagement represents another critical distinction of the digital age. In the era of print and television, information consumption was often confined to specific times and spaces—reading a book in a quiet study or watching the evening news in a living room.

Today, the ubiquity of smartphones and wearable devices ensures that information is accessible at any moment, eroding traditional boundaries between work, leisure, and rest. This perpetual accessibility exacerbates cognitive overload by eliminating opportunities for mental rest and recovery, a stark contrast to earlier periods where the absence of constant connectivity provided natural pauses for reflection and rejuvenation.

Despite these differences, the historical parallels underscore a fundamental truth: the human brain has consistently struggled to adapt to environments of information abundance. Each technological revolution has prompted a reevaluation of how individuals and societies manage cognitive resources. Just as Renaissance scholars developed organizational tools to navigate the deluge of printed texts, modern individuals must cultivate strategies to navigate the digital landscape. The historical perspective also highlights the cyclical nature of these challenges, suggesting that while the specifics of cognitive overload evolve, the underlying dynamics of human cognition and technological innovation remain enduringly intertwined.

Understanding the historical trajectory of cognitive overload offers valuable insights into the present crisis and potential paths forward. By recognizing that the current attention economy is not an unprecedented anomaly but rather the latest chapter in a long-standing struggle, it becomes possible to approach its challenges with a sense of perspective and resilience. As with past disruptions, the solution lies not in resisting technological progress but in developing adaptive strategies that align with the brain's natural capacities and limitations. The lessons of history remind us that while the tools may change, the need for thoughtful engagement with information is a constant, requiring vigilance, creativity, and a commitment to preserving the integrity of human cognition amidst the noise.

As we navigate the intricate interplay between human cognition and the relentless pace of technological change, the question arises: what makes the digital age uniquely challenging? Unlike past technological disruptions, where moments of stillness allowed for reflection and adaptation, today's digital landscape operates on a ceaseless cycle of engagement. The consequences of this shift ripple across every facet of life, shaping how we work, connect, and find meaning in an increasingly connected world. To understand how individuals and societies can reclaim agency in this environment, we must delve deeper into the mechanisms driving the digital attention economy and its profound influence on human behavior. The next section explores this uncharted terrain, examining how the commodification of attention reshapes not only our cognitive landscape but also the very fabric of our social and cultural existence.

Part 2: The Human Cost of Cognitive Overload

Neurological Consequences

The brain exists today in an environment it was never designed for, bombarded by a ceaseless stream of information, distractions, and demands for attention. From the moment we wake to the glow of a smartphone screen, our minds are immersed in an unrelenting cycle of stimuli—notifications, emails, social media updates, and endless streams of news. This constant engagement is more than a mere convenience of modern life; it is a profound disruption of the brain's natural rhythms.

In its evolutionary context, the human brain was optimized for focus. Survival depended on the ability to concentrate on singular tasks—tracking prey, gathering resources, or scanning the environment for potential threats. Cognitive energy was a finite and precious resource, expended judiciously. Yet today, the same mechanisms that allowed our ancestors to thrive in sparse, information-light environments are being exploited in a digital ecosystem designed to fragment attention and demand perpetual engagement. The very design of our modern technologies—from the instant gratification of notifications to the infinite allure of scrolling—leverages this cognitive mismatch, pulling us into a vortex of overstimulation.

This relentless flood of input places extraordinary demands on the brain's attentional system. The prefrontal cortex, responsible for managing focus, decision-making, and self-regulation, bears the brunt of this assault. Each shift of attention, whether to check a message or glance at a notification, drains cognitive resources and disrupts the flow of concentration. The result is a state of continuous partial attention, where the mind flits from one stimulus to the next without fully engaging in any of them. Over time, this constant toggling erodes the brain's ability to maintain sustained focus, leaving us cognitively fatigued and increasingly distracted.

The modern brain's overstimulation is not just a metaphorical strain but a measurable neurological phenomenon. Functional brain imaging reveals how the incessant demands on attention impair cognitive efficiency. Tasks that once required deep thought and reflection are now performed in fragmented bursts, leading to slower decision-making and diminished productivity. Cognitive overload—a state in which the sheer volume of information surpasses the brain's capacity to process it—has become a defining feature of contemporary life. This state leaves individuals overwhelmed, unable to retain information, and plagued by a persistent sense of mental clutter.

As this overstimulation persists, it sets off a feedback loop that reinforces its own effects. Each interaction with technology triggers a release of dopamine, the neurotransmitter associated with reward and pleasure. This creates a compulsion to engage further, as the brain craves the next hit of stimulation. Over time, the brain's reward pathways become overstimulated, leading to dysregulation and a diminished capacity for intrinsic motivation. The more we consume, the more our brains adapt to this heightened level of engagement, making it increasingly difficult to find satisfaction in less stimulating, more contemplative activities.

What we experience as overstimulation is not merely the byproduct of technological progress but the outcome of deliberate design. Features such as autoplay, infinite scrolling, and notification alerts are engineered to exploit our attentional vulnerabilities, ensuring that our focus remains captive. These mechanisms tap into the brain's innate biases, such as the tendency to seek novelty and avoid uncertainty, drawing us deeper into cycles of engagement. The overstimulated brain, therefore, is not just distracted—it is being reshaped, its neural pathways rewired by the constant demands placed upon it.

This reshaping has profound implications for cognitive health. Overstimulation weakens the brain's ability to adapt, diminishing its neuroplasticity—the capacity to form and reorganize synaptic connections in response to learning and experience. It impairs working memory, leaving us less equipped to retain and manipulate information. It also distorts the brain's dopamine system, driving compulsive behaviors and undermining emotional regulation. These effects, individually and collectively, compromise our ability to think deeply, act decisively, and engage meaningfully with the world around us.

The overstimulated brain is a brain in crisis, caught in a cycle of overuse and undernourishment. It is a mind constantly busy but rarely fulfilled, inundated with input yet starved of clarity. To break free from this cycle, we must first understand how it has come to dominate our cognitive lives and recognize the profound cost it exacts on our mental and emotional well-being. Only then can we begin the work of reclaiming our attention and restoring balance.

Neuroplasticity: The Brain's Adaptive Limits

The human brain is an extraordinary organ, capable of remarkable adaptability. Its capacity for neuroplasticity—the ability to form, strengthen, and reorganize neural connections in response to experience—underpins our learning, memory, and resilience. However, this adaptability is not boundless. When pushed to its limits by unrelenting cognitive demands, the brain begins to falter, revealing the fragile balance between its inherent flexibility and its structural constraints.

Constant stimulation, a hallmark of the modern digital era, challenges the brain's ability to adapt healthily. In environments of continuous novelty and distraction, neural pathways are repeatedly activated, reinforcing patterns that prioritize immediate engagement over long-term cognitive development. This creates a phenomenon known as maladaptive plasticity, where the brain's natural tendency to adapt leads to the reinforcement of unproductive or even harmful habits. Over time, the neural architecture becomes skewed toward short-term gratification, at the expense of skills like deep focus, problem-solving, and reflective thinking.

One critical area affected by these demands is working memory—the mental workspace where information is held temporarily for processing and manipulation. Working memory is finite, capable of handling only a limited amount of information at any given moment. Yet in a world of endless emails, notifications, and shifting tasks, this system is perpetually overloaded. The consequence is cognitive fragmentation, where the brain struggles to hold and integrate information, leading to errors, omissions, and an overall sense of mental clutter. Research shows that excessive multitasking, a behavior often necessitated by modern work and technology, reduces working memory capacity and disrupts the brain's ability to filter out irrelevant information.

This constant strain also taxes the brain's executive functions—processes governed by the prefrontal cortex that manage decision-making, impulse control, and attention regulation. Executive functions rely on periods of sustained mental effort interspersed with restorative breaks. When overstimulation becomes the norm, the brain loses these essential cycles of engagement and recovery. This leads to decision fatigue, where even minor choices feel overwhelming, and self-regulation falters. People become more prone to impulsive actions, procrastination, and difficulty prioritizing tasks, further exacerbating cognitive inefficiency.

Dopamine, a neurotransmitter central to the brain's reward system, plays a significant role in this dynamic. Each interaction with a source of novelty—whether a new social media post, a ping from a notification, or a breaking news alert—triggers a dopamine release, reinforcing the behavior and encouraging repetition. While this system evolved to promote survival behaviors, such as seeking food or social connection, the modern attention economy has co-opted it. The brain, unable to distinguish between genuine rewards and artificial stimulation, becomes locked in a cycle of seeking short bursts of gratification. Over time, this overstimulation blunts the brain's dopamine response, requiring ever greater stimulation to achieve the same level of reward. This desensitization undermines intrinsic motivation, making everyday tasks feel less satisfying and more effortful.

The effects of these adaptive limits extend beyond cognitive efficiency, influencing emotional regulation and stress responses. The overstimulated brain struggles to maintain equilibrium, oscillating between hyperarousal and mental exhaustion. This impairs the brain's ability to process emotions effectively, leading to heightened anxiety, irritability, and difficulty managing stress. Neuroimaging studies reveal that chronic overstimulation reduces activity in the medial prefrontal cortex—a region involved in emotional control and reflective thought—while heightening activity in the amygdala, the brain's center for fear and stress responses. This imbalance creates a feedback loop, where heightened stress further diminishes cognitive and emotional resources, compounding the challenges of overstimulation.

Ultimately, the brain's adaptive limits represent a cautionary boundary. While our neural systems are designed to respond dynamically to challenges, they are not invincible. Overstimulation strains the very mechanisms that enable us to thrive, impairing our capacity to learn, think critically, and maintain emotional balance. Recognizing and respecting these limits is essential for reclaiming mental clarity in an age that too often demands more than the brain can sustainably give.

WORKING MEMORY: THE COGNITIVE BOTTLENECK

Working memory, often described as the brain's mental workspace, is fundamental to human cognition. It allows us to temporarily hold and manipulate information, enabling tasks like problem-solving, decision-making, and planning. However, working memory is inherently limited, with most people capable of holding only a few discrete pieces of information at once. This limitation, often referred to as the "cognitive bottleneck," becomes particularly strained in the face of relentless demands for attention.

In the modern digital environment, working memory is constantly bombarded by streams of information. Emails, notifications, social media updates, and multitasking expectations conspire to exceed its natural capacity. Unlike long-term memory, which has an almost infinite storage potential, working memory is transient, designed for efficiency rather than endurance. When it is overloaded, the brain struggles to process and prioritize information, leading to errors, omissions, and an overwhelming sense of mental fatigue.

One consequence of this overload is cognitive fragmentation. The frequent interruptions that characterize modern life, such as a ping from a phone or a shifting task at work, force the brain to reset its focus repeatedly. Each shift consumes valuable cognitive resources, disrupting the neural coherence necessary for complex thinking. Studies reveal that after an interruption, it can take several minutes to regain full focus on a task, during which working memory operates less efficiently. Over time, this fragmentation reduces the brain's ability to integrate information cohesively, impairing both short-term performance and long-term learning.

Moreover, chronic overstimulation reconfigures how the brain allocates working memory resources. Repeated exposure to rapid, superficial information—such as scrolling through headlines or skimming social media feeds—trains the brain to favor speed over depth. This is sometimes referred to as "shallow processing," where the emphasis on immediate comprehension sacrifices deeper cognitive engagement. As a result, tasks that require sustained focus, such as analyzing complex problems or synthesizing diverse ideas, become more challenging. The capacity for deep work—a state of uninterrupted, high-concentration thinking—erodes under the constant strain of managing transient, low-value information.

This bottleneck effect is exacerbated by the phenomenon of multitasking. Despite its prevalence in modern workplaces and lifestyles, the human brain is fundamentally ill-suited for true multitasking. Instead, it engages in rapid task-switching, which imposes additional burdens on working memory. Each switch requires reorienting focus, suppressing irrelevant information from the previous task, and activating new neural circuits relevant to the next one. This process is cognitively expensive, consuming the limited bandwidth of working memory and reducing overall task efficiency. Research consistently shows that multitasking diminishes performance, increases error rates, and heightens stress—all clear manifestations of an overloaded cognitive system.

Beyond its immediate impacts, working memory overload also has cascading effects on other cognitive processes. Decision-making, for example, relies heavily on working memory to compare options, weigh potential outcomes, and integrate new information. When this mental workspace is overburdened, decisions become more impulsive or overly simplistic, as the brain defaults to heuristics or gut reactions to conserve energy. Similarly, creativity—a process that requires the blending of diverse ideas and the exploration of novel connections—suffers when working memory is consumed by trivial distractions.

To compound these challenges, the constant strain on working memory is not easily alleviated by rest or downtime. The brain's default mode network, which supports reflective thought and memory consolidation during rest, is often disrupted by digital distractions that prevent the kind of mental idleness necessary for recovery. Without opportunities for mental respite, the cognitive bottleneck becomes a chronic state, diminishing not only day-to-day functioning but also long-term cognitive resilience.

Understanding working memory as a bottleneck underscores the importance of managing cognitive load effectively. It is a reminder that the brain's capacity for processing information, while remarkable, is not infinite. By respecting these limits and cultivating environments that support focus and clarity, individuals can mitigate the strains of the attention economy and preserve their ability to think, decide, and create with depth and purpose.

DOPAMINE PATHWAYS: OVERSTIMULATION AND ADDICTION

Dopamine, often referred to as the brain's "reward molecule," plays a crucial role in motivation, learning, and reinforcement of behavior. It is the neurotransmitter that signals pleasure and reinforces actions that satisfy biological or psychological needs. In a balanced environment, dopamine pathways drive adaptive behaviors, encouraging exploration, effort, and the pursuit of meaningful goals. However, in the overstimulated landscape of the modern attention economy, these pathways are exploited and overactivated, leading to maladaptive patterns of dependence and addiction.

The overstimulation of dopamine pathways begins with the deliberate design of digital technologies to exploit the brain's reward system. Notifications, likes, retweets, and algorithmically curated content are engineered to deliver unpredictable, intermittent rewards. This unpredictability mirrors the reinforcement schedules seen in gambling, where the uncertainty of a payout creates a compelling loop of anticipation and reward. Each time we receive a notification or discover new content, our brains release a surge of dopamine, reinforcing the behavior that led to the reward. Over time, this trains us to seek these digital stimuli compulsively, prioritizing them over other, more balanced sources of satisfaction.

This constant engagement with reward-heavy stimuli alters the sensitivity of dopamine receptors in the brain. Repeated surges of dopamine can lead to desensitization, a process where the receptors become less responsive to the neurotransmitter. This reduced sensitivity necessitates greater levels of stimulation to achieve the same sense of reward, creating a cycle of escalating engagement and dependence. Activities that once provided natural dopamine boosts—such as reading a book, enjoying a meal, or engaging in face-to-face conversations—pale in comparison to the artificially amplified rewards of digital interactions.

Moreover, the focus on immediate, superficial rewards diminishes the brain's ability to sustain effort toward long-term goals. Dopamine is central to the brain's capacity for delayed gratification—the willingness to forego an immediate reward in favor of a larger, future one. In an environment dominated by instant notifications, on-demand entertainment, and rapid-fire updates, the neural pathways supporting patience and perseverance are underutilized. This can lead to a decline in the capacity for long-term planning and a preference for short-term, dopamine-driven gratification, with significant implications for productivity and personal growth.

The overstimulation of dopamine pathways also impacts emotional regulation. Dopamine is closely tied to the brain's pleasure-pain balance, influencing not only feelings of reward but also the aversion to its absence. When dopamine levels are frequently elevated, the brain compensates by increasing its sensitivity to pain signals, creating a rebound effect that manifests as irritability, restlessness, or low mood when stimulation is absent. This cycle, sometimes referred to as a "dopamine deficit state," makes it increasingly difficult to find satisfaction in daily life without constant external stimulation.

Furthermore, the interplay between dopamine and stress exacerbates the problem. Chronic overstimulation triggers the release of cortisol, the body's primary stress hormone, which interacts with dopamine systems to heighten feelings of urgency and reward-seeking. This coupling of stress and reward creates a feedback loop where individuals turn to dopamine-releasing activities as a way to cope with stress, even as these activities contribute to further stress by disrupting focus, sleep, and emotional balance.

The addictive nature of overstimulated dopamine pathways shares striking parallels with substance use disorders. Behavioral addictions, such as compulsive gaming or social media use, activate the same neural circuits as drugs like cocaine or nicotine. This explains why disengaging from these behaviors can lead to withdrawal-like symptoms, including anxiety, cravings, and a sense of emptiness. The neurological entrenchment of these patterns underscores the difficulty of breaking free from the cycle of digital dependence.

Recognizing the impact of overstimulated dopamine pathways is crucial for reclaiming agency in a world designed to hijack attention. It requires conscious efforts to recalibrate the brain's reward system, such as by fostering habits that provide intrinsic satisfaction, engaging in activities that demand focus without constant rewards, and imposing boundaries around the use of technologies that exploit dopamine-driven behaviors. By realigning dopamine pathways with sustainable and meaningful sources of reward, individuals can restore balance, resilience, and a deeper sense of fulfillment in their lives.

INTEGRATION OF EFFECTS: THE CUMULATIVE TOLL

The effects of cognitive overload, reduced neuroplasticity, diminished working memory, and overstimulation of dopamine pathways do not occur in isolation. Instead, they interact in complex and often compounding ways, exerting a cumulative toll on the brain's ability to function optimally. This integration of effects disrupts not only individual cognitive processes but also the broader architecture of mental resilience, emotional regulation, and overall well-being.

Fundamentally, cognitive overload creates a state of perpetual distraction that undermines the brain's ability to allocate resources efficiently. The neural energy required for higher-order thinking—tasks such as problem-solving, creativity, and reflective decision-making—is diverted toward managing an incessant influx of stimuli. This diversion weakens the brain's adaptive capacity, impairing neuroplasticity over time. As the neural networks responsible for attention and learning are repeatedly interrupted, their development stalls, creating a cognitive environment that favors superficial processing over deep understanding.

The strain on working memory further amplifies these challenges. Working memory acts as a cognitive bottleneck, holding and manipulating information essential for complex tasks. When this system is overloaded by constant stimulation, its capacity shrinks, leading to errors, inefficiency, and a diminished ability to synthesize information. The inability to retain and prioritize relevant data in working memory forces individuals into a reactive mode of thinking, where immediate responses take precedence over thoughtful deliberation. This reactive state reinforces impulsivity, which is further fueled by the overstimulation of dopamine pathways.

Dopamine, designed to reward goal-directed actions, becomes hijacked in this overstimulated environment, promoting compulsive engagement with short-term rewards at the expense of long-term objectives. This undermines the brain's ability to sustain focus and work toward meaningful, sustained achievements. The heightened demand for constant stimulation shifts the brain's reward baseline, making it harder to derive satisfaction from low-stimulation activities such as reading, meditating, or simply resting. Over time, this shift leads to chronic dissatisfaction, further exacerbating stress and emotional volatility.

The interplay between these effects also disrupts the brain's ability to regulate emotions effectively. The overstimulation of dopamine pathways contributes to a "feast-and-famine" cycle of emotional highs and lows, leaving individuals more susceptible to anxiety and mood swings. Meanwhile, the diminished capacity for focused reflection limits the brain's ability to process and manage stress constructively. This combination fosters a state of mental exhaustion, where even minor challenges can feel overwhelming due to the brain's depleted resources for coping and adaptation.

Sleep, one of the brain's most critical mechanisms for recovery and integration, becomes another casualty in this cumulative toll. The cognitive and emotional dysregulation caused by overstimulation interferes with the brain's ability to transition into restorative sleep states. Poor sleep quality further impairs neuroplasticity and working memory, creating a vicious cycle that deepens the impact of cognitive overload. The resulting sleep deprivation magnifies the negative effects on attention, learning, and emotional resilience, pushing the brain further into a state of chronic dysregulation.

On a larger scale, the integration of these effects has profound implications for overall well-being and productivity. Individuals caught in this cycle of overstimulation often struggle to maintain meaningful connections, both with others and with their own goals and aspirations. The inability to sustain deep focus and emotional stability erodes not only personal growth but also the capacity for collective problem-solving and societal progress.

The cumulative toll of these interconnected effects illustrates the urgent need for systemic and individual interventions. Addressing cognitive overload requires more than isolating individual symptoms—it demands a holistic approach that acknowledges how these effects reinforce one another. By fostering habits that support neuroplasticity, protecting working memory through mindful attention management, and recalibrating dopamine-driven behaviors, individuals can begin to reverse the cycle of overstimulation. This integrated recovery process can restore the brain's natural rhythms, enabling it to thrive in an environment that no longer dictates the terms of attention and focus.

The interplay of these neurological effects extends beyond the confines of individual cognition, setting the stage for far-reaching implications on personal well-being and societal dynamics. The cumulative toll of cognitive overload does not merely hinder memory or sap focus—it reshapes how we engage with the world around us. As overstimulated brains struggle to process the deluge of information, stress becomes a baseline state, leading to a ripple effect on emotional regulation, interpersonal relationships, and even public discourse. This transition from isolated neural consequences to broader psychological and societal disruptions underscores the gravity of the attention economy's impact. By understanding this bridge between the personal and the collective, we can begin to see why reclaiming cognitive balance is not just a private necessity but a cultural imperative.

THE OVERSTIMULATED BRAIN

Constant stimulation has transformed the modern brain into an environment of near-constant activity, with little reprieve from sensory, cognitive, and emotional inputs. This incessant engagement with digital devices, social platforms, and information streams imposes a relentless demand on the brain's neural systems, fundamentally altering its functioning. At the core of this transformation lies a heightened state of arousal, which has profound implications for neural pathways and the brain's adaptive mechanisms.

The brain's natural rhythms, designed for balance between periods of focus and rest, are disrupted by the continuous barrage of stimuli. Each notification, scroll, or video triggers a burst of neural activity, reinforcing pathways in the prefrontal cortex and limbic system that prioritize novelty and immediate gratification. This constant bombardment prevents the brain from returning to a baseline state of relaxation, fostering a feedback loop that perpetuates further engagement.

The overstimulated brain begins to rewire itself, favoring immediate, surface-level processing over the deep, reflective cognition it once prioritized. Key neural networks, such as the default mode network, which facilitates introspection and memory consolidation, are increasingly suppressed by the persistent focus on external inputs. Over time, this rewiring diminishes the brain's capacity for attentional control, leading to difficulties in filtering distractions and maintaining focus on single tasks.

Physiologically, this overstimulation taxes the brain's energy reserves, leading to mental fatigue and impaired cognitive resilience. Neural plasticity—the brain's ability to adapt, learn, and form new connections—becomes compromised as the brain prioritizes efficiency for responding to repetitive, low-level tasks over fostering long-term growth and creativity. This environment fosters a vicious cycle: overstimulation depletes the brain's resources, reducing its ability to manage further inputs, which then exacerbates cognitive overload.

The overstimulated brain, thus, is not merely a metaphor for modern life but a measurable shift in neural functioning. This shift underpins many of the challenges individuals face today, from difficulties in sustaining attention to heightened emotional reactivity. These changes, far from being benign, form the foundation for more profound disruptions in mental and physical well-being, which ripple through critical domains such as sleep, stress regulation, and emotional health. The implications of this transformation extend beyond individual experiences, hinting at broader societal consequences yet to be fully understood.

NEUROPLASTICITY: THE BRAIN'S ADAPTIVE LIMITS

Neuroplasticity, the brain's remarkable ability to reconfigure itself in response to experience, is both a cornerstone of human adaptability and a vulnerability in the era of constant stimulation. While this capacity enables learning and growth, it is not without limits. When inundated with perpetual stimuli, the brain's adaptive mechanisms are co-opted to prioritize short-term reactivity at the expense of long-term cognitive development. This maladaptive plasticity leads to structural and functional changes that challenge the brain's ability to thrive in complex environments.

In a balanced state, neuroplasticity supports the strengthening of synaptic connections associated with meaningful learning and problem-solving. However, under conditions of excessive stimulation—such as frequent interruptions by notifications or habitual multitasking—synaptic reinforcement shifts toward reactive pathways. The brain's resources are redirected to manage repetitive and immediate demands, resulting in a dominance of neural circuits that favor rapid, low-level responses over sustained, reflective thought. This phenomenon is particularly evident in the prefrontal cortex, where networks responsible for executive function and higher-order thinking struggle to maintain efficiency amidst the constant pull of external distractions.

Chronic overstimulation also disrupts the brain's capacity to prune redundant synaptic connections, a critical process for optimizing neural networks. Without adequate rest and recovery periods, the brain's ability to refine its architecture diminishes, leading to a state of neural clutter. This inefficiency undermines memory consolidation, decision-making, and the integration of new information, while fostering a sense of cognitive fog.

Moreover, the brain's reliance on plasticity to adapt to overstimulation comes with a hidden cost: the erosion of flexibility. As neural circuits repeatedly engage in superficial, stimulus-driven activities, they become entrenched, reducing the brain's capacity to shift gears or respond to novel and complex challenges. This rigidity is particularly concerning in younger individuals, whose brains are at their peak plasticity and thus highly susceptible to environmental shaping. The habitual engagement with shallow, fast-paced stimuli during critical developmental windows can have enduring consequences for attention, creativity, and emotional regulation.

While neuroplasticity is often celebrated as a universal asset, it is increasingly clear that its limits are being tested by modern lifestyles. The brain's adaptive potential, once a source of resilience, becomes a liability when channeled into unproductive or harmful patterns. These changes in neural architecture represent more than individual cognitive struggles; they signal a deeper, systemic shift in how humans engage with their environments, posing challenges that extend far beyond the personal sphere.

Working Memory: The Cognitive Bottleneck

Working memory, often described as the brain's "mental workspace," is a finite resource tasked with temporarily holding and manipulating information. It plays a crucial role in nearly every cognitive function, from problem-solving to decision-making. However, the constant barrage of information characteristic of the digital age places extraordinary demands on this limited system, creating what can be described as a cognitive bottleneck. This bottleneck impairs the brain's ability to process, prioritize, and retain information, with profound implications for both individual cognition and collective productivity.

Under normal circumstances, working memory effectively juggles a manageable number of mental tasks by maintaining a delicate balance between storage and processing. However, the modern environment of incessant notifications, fragmented tasks, and rapid information flow overwhelms this equilibrium. The brain's attentional resources are repeatedly diverted, forcing working memory to constantly reset and reallocate focus. This state of perpetual interruption depletes cognitive energy, leading to diminished task performance and an increased likelihood of errors.

One of the most insidious effects of this overstimulation is its impact on working memory's capacity. Research indicates that frequent task-switching—a behavior encouraged by digital multitasking—reduces the efficiency with which the brain encodes and retrieves information. Neural circuits responsible for maintaining focus are disrupted, resulting in a fragmented cognitive landscape where thoughts are incomplete and connections between ideas are weak. Over time, the brain begins to favor shallow, surface-level processing over the deeper, integrative thinking required for creativity and problem-solving.

Furthermore, excessive reliance on external tools, such as smartphones and search engines, compounds this decline in working memory. While these devices serve as convenient cognitive aids, they inadvertently weaken the brain's intrinsic capacity to hold and manipulate information. This phenomenon, often referred to as "cognitive offloading," creates a dependency that further erodes working memory's efficiency. Paradoxically, the very tools designed to enhance productivity may contribute to its decline by fostering a passive engagement with information.

The consequences of this bottleneck extend beyond diminished task performance. Impairments in working memory also affect emotional regulation and social interactions. When cognitive resources are stretched thin, individuals become more susceptible to impulsive decision-making and reactive behaviors. This lack of cognitive control not only exacerbates stress but also undermines the quality of interpersonal relationships, as the ability to remain present and engaged in conversation diminishes.

At a societal level, the strain on working memory is evident in declining attention spans and a collective inability to sustain focus on complex, long-term issues. From climate change to public health crises, the fragmented cognitive patterns fostered by modern lifestyles hinder the capacity for strategic thinking and coordinated action. The bottleneck in working memory, once an individual challenge, now represents a broader crisis of attention that demands urgent examination and intervention.

Working memory is a finite and vulnerable resource, uniquely susceptible to the demands of constant stimulation. Its decline in the face of cognitive overload highlights the importance of creating environments that support focus, encourage sustained attention, and reduce unnecessary distractions. Without such measures, the cumulative effects of this bottleneck will continue to compromise individual potential and societal progress alike.

INTEGRATION OF EFFECTS

The cumulative effects of reduced neuroplasticity, diminished working memory, and overstimulation of dopamine pathways converge to create a profound and multifaceted strain on the brain. While each of these mechanisms operates distinctly, their interplay results in a cascade of cognitive and emotional disruptions that amplify one another, underscoring the interconnected nature of neural processes. This integration of effects not only exacerbates individual challenges but also reveals how the modern environment compounds vulnerabilities within the brain's adaptive systems.

At the core of this cumulative toll is a fundamental breakdown in cognitive efficiency. Reduced neuroplasticity diminishes the brain's ability to adapt to new demands or recover from the damage caused by chronic overstimulation. Without the flexibility to form and reinforce new neural connections, the brain struggles to process and integrate the influx of information it faces daily. This rigidity heightens the strain on working memory, which is already compromised by constant interruptions and the expectation of multitasking. Together, these deficits create a vicious cycle: the inability to efficiently encode or recall information places greater demands on an already taxed working memory system, further eroding cognitive resilience.

Dopamine dysregulation exacerbates this cognitive strain by undermining the brain's motivational systems. Overexposure to intermittent rewards disrupts the delicate balance of the dopamine pathways, leading to compulsive behaviors that prioritize short-term gratification over sustained effort. This imbalance fosters habits that perpetuate cognitive overload, such as compulsive scrolling, frequent task-switching, or seeking novel stimuli, even at the expense of long-term goals. As a result, individuals become trapped in patterns of shallow engagement, where immediate rewards dominate, and deeper cognitive processes—such as critical thinking and problem-solving—are deprioritized.

Emotionally, these effects converge to heighten stress and diminish emotional regulation. Diminished working memory impairs the ability to process and contextualize emotional experiences, while dopamine overstimulation creates a heightened sensitivity to frustration and impulsivity. At the same time, reduced neuroplasticity limits the brain's capacity to develop adaptive coping mechanisms, leaving individuals more vulnerable to emotional exhaustion and burnout. The cumulative impact is a brain that is not only less efficient but also less resilient, perpetuating a state of cognitive and emotional fragility.

This integration of effects also extends to broader behavioral patterns, shaping how individuals interact with their environments and each other. Fragmented attention and diminished memory compromise the ability to engage in meaningful conversations, sustain collaborative efforts, or approach challenges with creativity and innovation. On a societal scale, these deficits manifest as reduced productivity, shallow engagement with complex issues, and an erosion of collective focus on long-term priorities.

The cumulative toll of these interconnected processes highlights the necessity of addressing cognitive overload at multiple levels. Individual strategies, such as prioritizing deep work, managing technology use, and practicing mindfulness, must be paired with systemic changes that promote healthier environments for cognitive function. Without such interventions, the integrated effects of these neural disruptions will continue to undermine both personal well-being and societal progress. Recognizing the synergistic nature of these challenges is the first step toward reclaiming agency over attention, focus, and emotional health in a world increasingly designed to exploit cognitive vulnerabilities.

TRANSITION TO BROADER IMPACTS

The interconnected effects of reduced neuroplasticity, diminished working memory, and overstimulation of dopamine pathways extend beyond the realm of individual cognition, reverberating into wider personal, social, and cultural dimensions. As these neural disruptions accumulate, they create a cascade of consequences that affect not only the brain's ability to function but also the very fabric of human interaction, creativity, and productivity. This transition from individual impacts to broader societal implications underscores the far-reaching influence of cognitive overload, revealing how the challenges faced by one person ripple outward to shape collective outcomes.

At the individual level, the inability to focus, retain information, or regulate emotions begins to erode the quality of daily experiences. These deficits disrupt personal relationships, as fragmented attention and emotional volatility diminish the capacity for empathy, patience, and meaningful communication. Socially, the collective impact becomes visible in a decline in collaborative problem-solving and a diminished ability to engage in deep, sustained discussions on complex issues. When focus is perpetually scattered, creativity and innovation falter, leaving individuals and groups less equipped to tackle challenges that demand long-term thinking and cooperation.

These neural deficits also have profound implications for institutions and societal structures. In professional contexts, cognitive overload manifests as reduced productivity, higher rates of burnout, and an erosion of workplace morale. Employees find themselves trapped in cycles of reactive behavior, constantly responding to immediate demands but struggling to engage in strategic planning or meaningful work. Educational systems, too, feel the strain, as both students and educators grapple with the effects of distraction and diminished cognitive resilience, compromising the depth and quality of learning.

Culturally, the overstimulated brain reshapes the way societies consume and engage with information. Shallow interactions with content—characterized by clickbait headlines, fleeting social media trends, and fragmented news cycles—replace nuanced analysis and critical engagement. This shift undermines the ability to address long-term challenges, from climate change to public health crises, as attention is diverted to ephemeral and emotionally charged stimuli. The cumulative effects reinforce cycles of polarization and misinformation, weakening the collective capacity for informed decision-making and reasoned discourse.

Transitioning from these cognitive and societal challenges to actionable solutions requires not only understanding the neurological roots of cognitive overload but also recognizing the systemic forces that perpetuate it. By addressing the broader implications of neural overstimulation, this exploration sets the stage for examining the ways in which individuals, communities, and institutions can reclaim focus and resilience in the attention economy. The transition from understanding the brain's vulnerabilities to tackling their societal consequences marks a critical juncture in the effort to mitigate the far-reaching impacts of cognitive overload.

THE DECLINE OF DEEP THINKING

The relentless pace of modern life, amplified by the digital age, has brought us into an era where cognitive overload is not merely a byproduct but a defining characteristic of our daily existence. Inundated with notifications, updates, and an endless stream of content, our minds struggle to keep pace with the demands placed upon them. This constant barrage of information does more than tire us; it fundamentally alters the way we think, process, and create. Cognitive overload has become a silent saboteur, eroding the mental faculties that once defined human ingenuity—creativity, problem-solving, and critical thinking. As we navigate this unrelenting storm of digital noise, the very tools we rely on for connection and productivity seem to be undermining the intellectual foundations that enable us to thrive.

At the heart of this challenge lies the concept of cognitive overload, a phenomenon where the human brain, limited in its capacity to process information, becomes overwhelmed by the sheer volume of stimuli. Unlike the occasional moments of stress that spur us into action, cognitive overload is persistent, draining our mental resources and leaving little room for reflection or innovation. The digital world, with its infinite scrolls and algorithmically curated feeds, thrives on fragmenting our attention, pulling us in countless directions at once. The result is a kind of mental fatigue that seeps into every aspect of our lives, dulling our ability to think deeply and critically.

The consequences of this overload are most acutely felt in our creative pursuits. Creativity demands space—mental and temporal—to allow ideas to incubate and connections to form. Yet, in a world where every moment is consumed by alerts or the compulsion to check our devices, this space is increasingly rare. The brain, overstimulated by constant inputs, struggles to shift into the state of mind necessary for divergent thinking, the cornerstone of innovation. What once might have been moments of serendipitous inspiration are now replaced by the frantic energy of multitasking, a mode of operation ill-suited to the complexities of creative thought.

Problem-solving, too, bears the brunt of cognitive overload. Effective problem-solving relies on a clear and focused mind, capable of synthesizing information and exploring various pathways to solutions. Yet, the fragmented nature of modern attention impairs these abilities, pushing us toward quicker, less thoughtful decisions. Instead of carefully weighing options and considering long-term outcomes, we resort to mental shortcuts and heuristics, which, while efficient in some contexts, often lead to errors and oversights. The quality of our problem-solving diminishes, and with it, our capacity to tackle the increasingly complex challenges of the world around us.

Perhaps most troubling is the erosion of critical thinking, the intellectual bedrock of informed decision-making and societal progress. In an environment saturated with competing narratives and misinformation, the ability to evaluate evidence, question assumptions, and form reasoned judgments is more vital than ever. Yet, cognitive overload undermines these processes, replacing deliberate analysis with reactive responses. The time and focus required to deeply engage with ideas are sacrificed to the immediacy of headlines and soundbites, leaving us vulnerable to manipulation and misjudgment. This decline in critical thinking is not merely an individual concern but a collective one, with implications for democracy, education, and the shared pursuit of knowledge.

These shifts in our cognitive abilities are not accidental; they are systemic, embedded in the very design of the digital ecosystems we inhabit. The interplay between technology and human cognition is complex, but one thing is clear: as we adapt to the demands of an overloaded world, the cost is not just personal—it is intellectual, cultural, and societal. The decline of creativity, problem-solving, and critical thinking marks a profound transformation in the way we engage with ourselves and the world, raising urgent questions about how we might reclaim the mental spaces needed to think deeply and act wisely.

UNDERSTANDING COGNITIVE OVERLOAD

Cognitive overload is not merely an abstract concept; it is a pervasive reality shaped by the very structure of the modern world. To understand its impact, one must first grasp how the human brain functions under normal conditions of information processing. Our cognitive systems are marvels of efficiency, capable of absorbing and interpreting vast amounts of data, but they are also finite. Working memory, the cognitive space where information is temporarily held and manipulated, operates with strict limitations. When the demands placed upon this system exceed its capacity, the result is overload—a state where the brain becomes overwhelmed and its ability to process, prioritize, and retain information is significantly impaired.

The digital age has amplified the conditions that lead to cognitive overload. Our devices are not passive tools but active participants in capturing and holding attention. Notifications, alerts, and algorithmically tailored content act as continuous interruptions, fragmenting our focus and pulling our minds in competing directions. Unlike the occasional distractions of the pre-digital era, these stimuli are relentless, designed to exploit our natural tendencies toward novelty and instant gratification. This perpetual state of engagement taxes the brain's resources, leaving little room for the deeper, more deliberate forms of thinking that underpin creativity, problem-solving, and critical analysis.

One of the most insidious effects of cognitive overload is its impact on memory, a foundational element of human cognition. Effective memory formation relies on the brain's ability to encode information into long-term storage, a process that requires both attention and repetition. Yet, in a state of overload, information is often processed superficially, if at all, leading to fragmented recall and an inability to draw connections between ideas. This not only hampers learning but also stifles the creative process, which depends on the ability to combine disparate pieces of knowledge in novel and meaningful ways.

Decision-making, another critical cognitive function, also suffers under the weight of overload. Faced with an overwhelming amount of information, the brain resorts to shortcuts, prioritizing speed over accuracy. While heuristics can be effective in familiar situations, they often lead to flawed judgments in complex or unfamiliar contexts. Over time, the cumulative effects of these impaired decisions can ripple outward, affecting not only individual outcomes but also broader societal dynamics, from workplace efficiency to public policy. The cognitive toll is compounded by the emotional strain of constantly navigating a world of competing demands, further diminishing our capacity to think clearly and act decisively.

To fully understand cognitive overload, it is essential to recognize that its effects are not confined to individual experiences. The broader societal implications are profound, shaping how we engage with information, interact with others, and address collective challenges. The fragmentation of attention fosters a culture of surface-level engagement, where depth and nuance are sacrificed for speed and volume. In such a context, the decline of deep thinking is not just a loss for individuals but for society as a whole, undermining our ability to innovate, collaborate, and solve the pressing issues of our time. Cognitive overload, then, is not merely a symptom of the digital age but a defining challenge, demanding a reexamination of how we live, work, and think in an increasingly complex world.

CREATIVITY AND OVERLOAD

Creativity thrives in the mental spaces where structure dissolves, and disparate ideas intermingle. These spaces are cultivated not through relentless focus or constant task-switching but in the freedom of mind-wandering—those moments when the brain meanders without a defined goal, stumbling upon connections that more deliberate thinking cannot achieve. Overstimulation, the hallmark of the digital age, has increasingly robbed individuals of this fertile ground for creativity. The perpetual barrage of notifications, emails, and algorithmically tailored content not only fragments attention but also disallows the brain the opportunity to rest in a state of productive idleness. This state, known as the "default mode network," is essential for the integrative thinking that underpins creative breakthroughs.

Studies in cognitive neuroscience have repeatedly shown that creativity is not born in the midst of endless tasks but rather in the intervals between them. The very structure of overstimulation suppresses these intervals. Each ping or buzz pulls the brain into reactive states, where immediate tasks override broader reflection. Constant task-switching, often mistaken for productivity, further compounds the problem by overloading working memory and diminishing cognitive flexibility. Flexibility—the capacity to see problems from novel angles—is a cornerstone of creativity. Yet, it falters under conditions of cognitive overload, as the brain becomes trapped in rigid patterns of response dictated by urgency rather than ingenuity.

Empirical evidence underscores the cost of this overstimulation. A longitudinal study published in the *Journal of Experimental Psychology* tracked the creative output of individuals in high-distraction environments compared to those with extended periods of undisturbed time. The findings were stark: those in uninterrupted settings produced ideas that were more original, complex, and interconnected. By contrast, the high-distraction group generated work that was derivative and fragmented. Similarly, experiments with task-switching have shown that it takes the brain significant time to regain focus and re-enter a creative "flow" state once interrupted, further highlighting how multitasking inhibits the depth necessary for meaningful ideation.

The repercussions of suppressed creativity extend beyond individual productivity to societal innovation. History is replete with examples of transformative ideas arising during periods of quiet reflection rather than incessant engagement. Albert Einstein famously conceived the theory of relativity while daydreaming, and countless artistic and scientific breakthroughs have emerged during states of mental wandering. Yet, the overstimulation of the digital age has created an environment hostile to such moments. Innovation, which once relied on the serendipity of unstructured thought, now competes with algorithms that direct attention outward rather than inward.

To combat this, individuals and institutions must reclaim the conditions that nurture creativity. Strategies like designated "no-device zones," intentional periods of disengagement, and the cultivation of boredom as a deliberate practice can restore the mental landscapes necessary for creative thought. Equally important is a cultural shift that redefines productivity—not as relentless busyness but as a balanced rhythm that honors the interplay of focused work and unstructured reflection. Without such interventions, the suppression of creativity under the weight of cognitive overload risks not only individual stagnation but also a collective decline in innovation and progress.

PROBLEM-SOLVING CHALLENGES

Problem-solving, a cornerstone of human intelligence, requires a harmonious interplay of attention, critical analysis, and the ability to synthesize disparate pieces of information into coherent solutions. However, in the age of cognitive overload, this intricate process is disrupted at every stage, undermining our capacity to approach problems with clarity and precision. The endless stream of information that characterizes modern life creates a state of perpetual distraction, leaving us unable to focus long enough to define problems accurately, let alone solve them effectively.

One of the key barriers posed by cognitive overload is the fragmentation of attention. Solving complex problems demands sustained focus, as the brain must hold multiple variables in mind while iteratively testing potential solutions. Yet, in a digital landscape designed to capture and divert our attention, the ability to concentrate for extended periods is steadily eroding. Notifications, multitasking, and the allure of instant gratification condition our minds to flit from one stimulus to the next, creating an environment where deep, sustained thinking becomes an increasingly rare experience.

Moreover, the quality of the information we engage with further compounds the problem. Algorithms that prioritize engagement over accuracy often serve up content that reinforces existing biases or presents overly simplistic solutions to nuanced issues. This fosters a cognitive environment where the complexity of real-world problems is overshadowed by the superficial allure of quick fixes. As a result, the skills necessary for effective problem-solving—such as critical thinking, analytical reasoning, and the ability to weigh competing perspectives—are gradually dulled, leaving us ill-prepared to navigate challenges that demand nuanced understanding.

Cognitive overload also affects our emotional regulation, which plays a crucial role in problem-solving. Effective solutions require not just intellectual engagement but also the ability to manage frustration, uncertainty, and the fear of failure. In an overstimulated mind, emotional resilience is often compromised, leading to hasty decisions driven by stress or anxiety rather than careful deliberation. The constant need to process information leaves little bandwidth for reflective thought, pushing individuals toward reactive rather than strategic responses to challenges.

Compounding these individual challenges are the societal implications of diminished problem-solving capacities. In an interconnected world where global issues such as climate change, public health, and geopolitical tensions demand collective action, the erosion of problem-solving skills becomes a shared vulnerability. The inability to engage in sustained critical thinking undermines collaborative efforts, leading to fragmented responses that fail to address the root causes of complex problems. As public discourse becomes increasingly polarized and reactionary, the collective capacity to solve shared challenges diminishes, threatening progress on critical fronts.

Recognizing the profound impact of cognitive overload on problem-solving is essential for addressing this growing crisis. By understanding how fragmented attention, biased information, and emotional dysregulation impede our ability to think deeply and act decisively, we can begin to reclaim the cognitive space needed for effective solutions. This reclamation is not merely an individual endeavor but a societal imperative, demanding a shift toward environments that foster focus, resilience, and the collaborative spirit necessary for tackling the challenges of our time.

CRITICAL THINKING UNDER THREAT

Critical thinking, the deliberate analysis and evaluation of information to form a reasoned judgment, is under siege in the age of cognitive overload. This essential intellectual tool thrives on clarity, depth, and time—qualities increasingly scarce in a world saturated with fragmented, rapid-fire content. As we navigate the ceaseless barrage of notifications, updates, and algorithm-curated feeds, the reflective space necessary for critical thinking contracts, leaving little room for questioning assumptions, analyzing arguments, or drawing well-supported conclusions.

At the heart of this decline is the transformation of how information is consumed and processed. In the past, engaging with complex issues often required deliberate effort—reading dense texts, debating ideas, or engaging in thoughtful discourse. Today, digital platforms prioritize immediacy over depth, encouraging users to skim headlines, react emotionally, and move on. This shift fosters a cognitive environment where surface-level understanding replaces nuanced insight, making it easier to accept information at face value rather than subjecting it to rigorous scrutiny. Critical thinking, which relies on the capacity to pause, evaluate, and question, struggles to flourish in such an ephemeral landscape.

Bias amplification is another casualty of this cognitive shift. Algorithms, designed to maximize engagement, serve content that aligns with existing preferences, creating echo chambers that reinforce preexisting beliefs. The result is a diminished capacity to entertain opposing viewpoints or reexamine one's own biases—both critical components of a well-developed critical thinking skillset. When individuals are consistently exposed to affirming rather than challenging ideas, their ability to assess the validity of diverse arguments weakens, fostering intellectual rigidity and polarization.

Cognitive overload also undermines the essential step of synthesis in critical thinking. Analyzing multiple perspectives and integrating them into a cohesive understanding requires mental bandwidth and focused attention, both of which are eroded by the constant demand to process new information. This is particularly evident in how people approach complex societal issues, where the sheer volume of data and conflicting narratives can overwhelm the mind's capacity to discern patterns and prioritize relevance. In such cases, individuals may resort to simplistic explanations or defer to authoritative voices without engaging in deeper analysis, further eroding the critical faculties needed for informed decision-making.

Furthermore, the emotional toll of cognitive overload has profound implications for critical thinking. Feelings of stress, frustration, or anxiety often accompany the relentless processing of information, leaving little room for the calm and measured thought required for reasoned evaluation. Emotional responses to content—be it outrage, fear, or exhilaration—are frequently amplified by digital platforms that exploit psychological triggers. These heightened emotions can cloud judgment, skew perceptions, and lead to impulsive reactions, further distancing individuals from the rational and reflective processes at the core of critical thinking.

The societal implications of diminished critical thinking are far-reaching. Democracies depend on an informed and discerning populace capable of evaluating policies, leaders, and media narratives. When the capacity for critical thought is weakened, public discourse becomes more susceptible to manipulation, propaganda, and demagoguery. Decisions made in such a context are more likely to reflect collective impulsivity than collective wisdom, undermining the very foundations of rational governance and progress.

Restoring critical thinking in an age of cognitive overload requires conscious effort and systemic change. It calls for reclaiming reflective spaces, prioritizing depth over speed in information consumption, and fostering environments that challenge biases while encouraging intellectual humility. By doing so, individuals can regain the capacity to think critically and society can safeguard this invaluable tool against the corrosive effects of the digital age.

EMPIRICAL EXAMPLES

Empirical examples bring into sharp focus how cognitive overload undermines critical thinking in real-world contexts, exposing vulnerabilities that ripple through personal decisions and societal outcomes. Consider the widespread prevalence of misinformation during critical events, such as the COVID-19 pandemic. The onslaught of data—from official guidelines and scientific studies to conspiratorial social media posts—created an environment of information saturation. The sheer volume overwhelmed many individuals, leaving them ill-equipped to discern credible sources from dubious ones. This led to widespread misunderstandings, ranging from vaccine hesitancy fueled by cherry-picked data to public health measures dismissed based on misinterpreted evidence. Such cases exemplify how cognitive overload hampers the ability to critically evaluate and synthesize information when it matters most.

The political realm provides another striking example. During election cycles, social media platforms are inundated with campaign advertisements, sensational headlines, and algorithmically prioritized content designed to capture attention. This deluge often emphasizes emotional appeal over substantive policy discussions, encouraging snap judgments and polarizing rhetoric. The 2016 U.S. presidential election saw significant interference through the dissemination of false or misleading information on platforms like Facebook. Research later revealed that such content was far more likely to be shared and believed than factual reports, highlighting how cognitive overload can lead to reliance on heuristics and emotional cues rather than thoughtful analysis. In this landscape, critical thinking is sacrificed for immediacy, with profound consequences for democratic processes.

The corporate sector illustrates yet another dimension of this challenge. Professionals navigating high-pressure work environments often face a constant influx of emails, notifications, and tasks, leaving little time for reflective problem-solving. One notable study found that employees in "always-on" cultures reported lower creativity and decision-making quality, as their cognitive resources were consumed by reactive multitasking rather than proactive, strategic thinking. This erosion of critical faculties is not just a personal issue but a systemic one, affecting innovation, productivity, and long-term organizational success. The inability to step back and critically evaluate processes or solutions stems directly from cognitive overload's debilitating effects.

Educational settings further underscore this dynamic, as students increasingly struggle to develop critical thinking skills amidst the distractions of digital learning environments. For instance, studies have shown that students who frequently multitask with social media while studying or attending online lectures retain less information and perform worse in critical analysis tasks. The constant toggling between academic content and external stimuli fragments attention and diminishes the mental discipline required for deep engagement with complex material. This has led educators to rethink instructional strategies, emphasizing the need to create environments that shield learners from overload and foster sustained focus.

The economic and social consequences of diminished critical thinking manifest starkly in consumer behavior. Algorithm-driven advertising exploits cognitive overload by presenting tailored recommendations that cater to immediate desires rather than encouraging deliberate consideration of choices. From impulsive online purchases to the normalization of predatory lending practices, the inability to critically evaluate the long-term implications of decisions has far-reaching consequences. These examples underscore how cognitive overload skews judgment, reinforcing patterns that prioritize short-term gratification over reasoned and ethical decision-making.

Empirical evidence thus reveals the multifaceted ways in which cognitive overload undermines critical thinking across domains. Whether in health, politics, work, education, or consumer behavior, the examples highlight a consistent pattern: as the cognitive demands of modern life exceed human capacity, the reflective and evaluative processes essential to critical thought are compromised, with individual and collective costs that cannot be ignored. Addressing these challenges requires not only individual awareness but systemic interventions to mitigate the overwhelming influx of information and prioritize the cultivation of critical faculties.

SYSTEMIC IMPLICATIONS

The systemic implications of cognitive overload's assault on creativity, problem-solving, and critical thinking extend far beyond individual experiences, infiltrating institutions and societal structures with profound and often insidious consequences. At its core, the erosion of these cognitive capabilities undermines the foundational mechanisms that drive progress, equity, and innovation, creating a landscape where reactive behaviors dominate and reflective, long-term strategies fall by the wayside.

In governance, the inability to foster critical discourse and collective decision-making has systemic repercussions. Policies addressing complex issues like climate change, healthcare reform, or social justice rely on a population capable of engaging with nuanced, data-driven arguments. Yet, the cognitive overload imposed by fragmented media narratives and relentless digital stimuli creates an environment in which superficial soundbites often overshadow meaningful debate. Lawmakers, influenced by the same forces, may prioritize optics over substance, enacting short-sighted legislation that fails to address root causes. This erosion of critical engagement feeds into a cyclical dynamic, where public and political decisions become increasingly disconnected from evidence-based reasoning.

In the corporate sector, the systemic effects of diminished problem-solving and innovation capacities threaten economic sustainability. Organizations depend on teams capable of navigating ambiguity, adapting to change, and envisioning transformative solutions. Yet, the inundation of data and constant connectivity that characterizes modern work environments fosters a culture of immediacy, where decisions are driven by short-term metrics and surface-level analysis. This results in missed opportunities for innovation, as employees lack the cognitive bandwidth to engage deeply with challenges or anticipate future trends. The systemic impact is an economy less equipped to compete in an era where adaptability and creativity are paramount.

Educational systems, too, bear the weight of these systemic challenges. As cognitive overload compromises students' ability to focus, analyze, and think critically, it also diminishes the pipeline of future leaders, innovators, and informed citizens. Institutions face increasing pressure to redesign curricula and learning environments that can counteract the effects of digital distractions. However, systemic inertia and resource constraints often result in piecemeal solutions that fail to address the underlying issues comprehensively. The ripple effect is a society less prepared to grapple with the complexities of a rapidly evolving world.

Media ecosystems amplify these systemic implications by perpetuating cycles of distraction and cognitive overload. Algorithmically curated content favors sensationalism, controversy, and rapid consumption, eroding the space for in-depth analysis and thoughtful critique. This systemic prioritization of engagement metrics over informational value weakens the public sphere, where informed debate and collective problem-solving should flourish. As media platforms increasingly shape public opinion, their role in exacerbating the cognitive crisis becomes a societal liability with far-reaching implications for democracy, culture, and community cohesion.

The systemic implications of cognitive overload extend to public health. The mental strain caused by chronic information saturation is linked to rising rates of stress, anxiety, and burnout, creating a public health crisis that burdens healthcare systems and undermines societal well-being. The diminished capacity for critical thinking and problem-solving exacerbates health disparities, as individuals struggle to navigate complex healthcare systems or discern credible information about their conditions. This perpetuates cycles of inequality, where those most affected by cognitive overload are also the least equipped to access the resources needed to mitigate its effects.

Addressing these systemic challenges requires a paradigm shift that recognizes cognitive overload as not just an individual concern but a societal issue demanding collective action. Policies promoting digital literacy, ethical media practices, and work-life balance are crucial, as are structural changes in education, governance, and corporate culture. Without such interventions, the systemic erosion of creativity, problem-solving, and critical thinking risks entrenching a world where complexity overwhelms capacity, leaving society ill-equipped to navigate its most pressing challenges.

The Quiet Disappearance

There was a time when boredom was not a state to escape but an inevitable companion of human existence. In the quiet moments between events, when distractions were few and time seemed to stretch endlessly, boredom often took root. It was uncomfortable, to be sure, but it also served as fertile ground for innovation, self-reflection, and creativity. Philosophers like Kierkegaard contemplated its existential weight, and countless artists, writers, and thinkers credited their most profound breakthroughs to those idle hours when their minds were left to wander. Boredom, it seemed, was not merely a void but a catalyst for discovery.

In the modern world, however, boredom has become an endangered state. The rise of digital technologies has transformed every moment of stillness into an opportunity for engagement. Smartphones, streaming platforms, and social media have colonized the once-empty spaces of our lives, offering endless content and connectivity at our fingertips. Even waiting in line or riding an elevator no longer necessitates a confrontation with our thoughts; a quick scroll through a screen fills the void. This shift has been so seamless that many of us hardly recognize what we have lost in the process.

What happens to a mind that is never bored? Without those moments of discomfort that compel us to look inward or reach outward for inspiration, do we lose a part of our creative and intellectual potential? To answer these questions, we must first understand the role boredom once played in shaping human thought and innovation. Its disappearance is not just a cultural shift but a profound alteration in the cognitive rhythms that have long defined our species.

As we examine this transformation, it becomes clear that the erasure of boredom has consequences far beyond individual creativity. It impacts how we solve problems, how we process the world around us, and how we connect with ourselves. The loss of this once-common state demands not only reflection but also a reimagining of how we engage with the ever-present forces vying for our attention.

BOREDOM AS A CATALYST FOR CREATIVITY

In the history of human thought, boredom has been an unlikely yet powerful driver of creativity and innovation. When external stimuli are scarce, the mind turns inward, embarking on a journey of reflection and imagination. This introspective process, unencumbered by distraction, allows for the formation of new ideas and the exploration of uncharted mental territories. It is during these moments of cognitive wandering that many of humanity's greatest innovations have emerged. Artists, inventors, and thinkers often describe periods of profound boredom as preludes to their most transformative breakthroughs, where the absence of external engagement forces the mind to cultivate its inner resources.

The connection between boredom and creativity lies in the way the brain processes information when it is untethered from immediate demands. Studies in cognitive psychology suggest that boredom activates the brain's default mode network—a system associated with daydreaming, memory consolidation, and creative problem-solving. Unlike focused, goal-oriented thought, which is limited to solving immediate challenges, the default mode network encourages divergent thinking, where seemingly unrelated ideas connect in novel ways. It is a process akin to letting the pieces of a puzzle fall into place, often without conscious effort.

This relationship is not merely anecdotal but empirically supported. In one experiment, participants tasked with completing mundane activities such as reading a phone book were subsequently better at generating creative ideas than those who were not bored. The tedium appeared to prime their minds for imaginative leaps, illustrating the paradoxical value of boredom as a springboard for innovation. In the absence of external entertainment, the brain seeks novelty internally, creating solutions and narratives that might not have emerged otherwise.

However, in the attention economy, opportunities for such cognitive wanderings are increasingly rare. The constant influx of digital stimuli preempts the idleness necessary for the mind to engage in this deeper, more creative mode of thinking. Apps and algorithms are designed to capture every fragment of spare attention, transforming potential moments of boredom into monetizable interactions. As a result, the brain becomes habituated to external engagement, losing its capacity for the kind of self-directed creativity that boredom once nurtured.

The disappearance of boredom has profound implications for how we innovate and problem-solve as individuals and as a society. Without the cognitive space boredom provides, we risk becoming reactive rather than inventive, consumed by immediate concerns instead of envisioning broader possibilities. The challenge lies in reclaiming this lost state, not as an inconvenience to be avoided but as a vital component of the human experience, essential for fostering the creativity that drives progress and meaning in our lives.

PSYCHOLOGICAL MECHANICS OF BOREDOM

Boredom is often dismissed as a trivial discomfort, yet its psychological underpinnings reveal a complex interplay of neural and emotional processes. At the very essence, boredom arises when there is a mismatch between the brain's need for stimulation and the availability or perceived value of stimuli in the environment. This gap triggers an aversive state that pushes individuals to seek novelty, engagement, or meaning—a survival mechanism deeply embedded in human psychology. Far from being a passive emotion, boredom acts as a cognitive signal, nudging us toward exploration and growth.

Neuroscience sheds light on how boredom operates within the brain. The feeling is closely tied to activity in the brain's dopamine system, which governs motivation and reward. When environmental stimuli fail to meet expectations or provide anticipated rewards, dopamine levels drop, creating a sense of dissatisfaction. This neurological "itch" propels individuals to seek more fulfilling activities. Paradoxically, this state of dissatisfaction can be highly productive when allowed to run its course, as it fosters curiosity and the drive to resolve cognitive dissonance.

Psychologically, boredom challenges the mind to confront its aversion to stillness. In an overstimulated society, the discomfort of boredom often feels intolerable, leading to a compulsion to escape through immediate distractions like smartphones or social media. However, when individuals resist this urge to fill every moment, boredom can trigger introspection. The absence of external stimulation encourages the mind to generate its own content, a process that can lead to self-discovery, problem-solving, or the development of innovative ideas. In essence, boredom forces the brain to turn inward, drawing from its internal resources rather than relying on external input.

Modern research highlights boredom's dual nature: while it can foster creativity and resilience, it also has the potential to exacerbate feelings of emptiness or frustration if not channeled effectively. Long-term exposure to boredom without meaningful outlets can lead to maladaptive behaviors, such as substance abuse or compulsive screen time, as individuals seek to escape the discomfort. This duality underscores the importance of understanding and harnessing boredom rather than simply avoiding it.

In the context of the attention economy, the psychological mechanics of boredom are particularly relevant. Platforms that provide endless streams of content effectively hijack boredom's natural function, preventing the brain from engaging in the deeper, reflective states that boredom facilitates. By constantly pacifying the desire for novelty, these platforms suppress the creative and self-reflective potential boredom holds. To reclaim this lost opportunity, individuals must consciously resist the impulse to seek immediate gratification, allowing the discomfort of boredom to act as a catalyst for meaningful engagement and growth.

The Age of Instant Gratification

The age of instant gratification has fundamentally altered our relationship with boredom, transforming it from a natural and necessary aspect of human experience into an almost obsolete inconvenience. In a world where answers are a click away, entertainment streams endlessly, and social interactions occur at the push of a button, the time required for reflective pauses and creative incubation has been drastically shortened. This environment not only minimizes the space boredom occupies but also rewires our expectations for how we engage with the world, leading to a persistent craving for immediacy and stimulation.

At the heart of this transformation is the unprecedented accessibility of digital distractions. Platforms are designed to deliver dopamine hits on demand, whether through the excitement of a new notification, the satisfaction of a quick online purchase, or the ease of binge-watching a series. This constant availability of low-effort rewards creates a cycle of dependency, where the brain becomes increasingly reliant on external stimuli to feel engaged. Over time, the ability to tolerate the discomfort of boredom erodes, as the instinct to seek distraction becomes almost reflexive.

This shift has profound implications for cognitive and emotional development. Boredom, once a doorway to deeper thought, now feels like a void to be filled as quickly as possible. The decline in moments of unstructured time means fewer opportunities for creative problem-solving, introspection, and emotional processing. Without the space boredom provides, individuals are less likely to engage in the mental wandering that often leads to breakthroughs or profound insights. Instead, their cognitive energies are consumed by surface-level interactions with digital content, which offer immediate satisfaction but little lasting enrichment.

The societal impact of this trend is equally significant. As people grow less comfortable with boredom, there is a cultural drift toward superficial engagement and impatience. Long-term goals, which require sustained effort and delayed gratification, become harder to pursue in a landscape dominated by instant results. The erosion of boredom as a natural state undermines the resilience and persistence needed for complex problem-solving, both on a personal and societal level. In fields like education, innovation, and public discourse, the preference for quick fixes over enduring challenges stifles progress.

The age of instant gratification has redefined how we navigate the discomfort of idle moments, substituting quick rewards for the transformative potential of boredom. To reclaim this lost potential, individuals must consciously resist the pull of immediacy, embracing instead the uneasy yet fertile ground of waiting. It is within these pauses that true creativity, growth, and self-awareness are cultivated—a process now endangered in a world that promises everything instantly.

THE LOSS OF REFLECTIVE SPACES

The loss of reflective spaces in the modern era represents one of the most profound casualties of our increasingly overstimulated lives. Historically, reflective spaces were built into the fabric of daily existence—moments of solitude during a walk, quiet evenings without screens, or the natural lulls that encouraged contemplation. These intervals provided the mental room necessary for individuals to process their experiences, synthesize new ideas, and engage with their inner thoughts. Today, however, the pervasive reach of digital devices and the omnipresence of distractions have eroded these sanctuaries, leaving little room for meaningful reflection.

The disappearance of these spaces is closely tied to the constant connectivity afforded by technology. Mobile devices, with their endless notifications and on-demand content, transform even the most solitary moments into opportunities for external engagement. Waiting in line, sitting on a train, or even relaxing at home—formerly prime opportunities for introspection—are now filled with scrolling through feeds or checking emails. This perpetual activity fragments attention, preventing the deep and uninterrupted thinking that reflective spaces once fostered.

Moreover, the cultural valorization of productivity exacerbates the decline of reflective spaces. In a society that equates busyness with value, taking time to pause and think can feel like an indulgence rather than a necessity. The result is a relentless pressure to fill every moment with measurable output or visible engagement, further sidelining the unstructured mental wandering that sparks creativity and emotional clarity. This shift not only deprives individuals of personal growth but also diminishes the collective intellectual and cultural depth that emerges from sustained reflection.

The consequences of this loss extend beyond the individual level, affecting broader social dynamics. Without reflective spaces, the ability to engage deeply with complex issues is compromised. People are less likely to challenge their assumptions, explore nuanced perspectives, or grapple with ambiguity. This deficit in reflective thinking fuels polarization and superficial discourse, as quick opinions replace thoughtful deliberation. Societies that neglect reflection risk stagnation, as they fail to nurture the innovative and critical capacities necessary for addressing long-term challenges.

Recovering reflective spaces in this hyperconnected world demands intentional effort. It requires redefining the value of quiet moments and reclaiming them from the grip of constant stimulation. Whether through dedicated periods of screen-free time, practices like journaling and meditation, or simply allowing oneself to sit with thoughts unhurriedly, the act of carving out reflective spaces is an act of resistance. In doing so, individuals can reconnect with their inner selves and contribute to a culture that values depth over distraction, ensuring that the power of reflection endures in an age that too often neglects it.

TOWARDS A NEW RELATIONSHIP WITH BOREDOM

Moving toward a renewed relationship with boredom involves a conscious recognition of its transformative potential in a world that increasingly undervalues stillness. Boredom, once dismissed as a dull and undesirable state, is in fact a fertile ground for creative breakthroughs, emotional processing, and profound self-discovery. Reimagining our engagement with boredom requires not only a shift in individual attitudes but also systemic changes in how society prioritizes time and attention.

At an individual level, cultivating a new perspective on boredom begins with reframing it as an opportunity rather than an inconvenience. This involves resisting the urge to immediately fill idle moments with distractions, such as reaching for a phone or opening a new tab. Instead, these moments can be viewed as invitations to let the mind wander, embracing the discomfort as a prelude to deeper insight. Research in neuroscience suggests that allowing the brain to enter this unfocused state facilitates connections between disparate ideas, often leading to creative and innovative outcomes. By leaning into boredom, individuals can unlock its latent potential as a catalyst for intellectual and emotional growth.

On a broader scale, societal attitudes toward productivity and downtime must also evolve. In cultures that glorify perpetual activity, boredom is often stigmatized as wasted time rather than a necessary phase of mental regeneration. Changing this narrative involves promoting practices that honor unstructured time as a vital aspect of human development. Schools, workplaces, and public institutions can play a role by encouraging policies and environments that value deep thinking and reflective pauses. For instance, integrating moments of silence into daily routines or reducing the emphasis on multitasking can help normalize the experience of constructive boredom.

Rebuilding a healthier relationship with boredom also requires addressing the structural barriers posed by technology. Digital platforms are specifically engineered to capture attention, making it difficult to disengage and embrace stillness. Setting boundaries with technology—such as designated screen-free zones or digital detox periods—can create space for boredom to resurface naturally. Moreover, advocating for ethical design practices that prioritize user well-being over constant engagement is critical to counteracting the systemic forces that diminish opportunities for reflective boredom.

Redefining our relationship with boredom is about reclaiming autonomy over our inner lives. It challenges the pervasive narrative that equates busyness with worth and instead celebrates the introspective power of stillness. As individuals and societies learn to welcome boredom as a teacher rather than a nuisance, they open the door to richer creativity, deeper understanding, and a renewed sense of connection with both themselves and the world. In embracing boredom, we not only safeguard our mental and emotional health but also foster the conditions necessary for genuine progress and fulfillment in an increasingly distracted age.

SOCIETAL IMPLICATIONS

The fragmentation of individual attention is not an isolated phenomenon but one that reverberates through society, creating far-reaching consequences. What begins as a personal struggle to manage distractions ultimately scales into collective dysfunction, destabilizing social systems and institutions. The digital environment, designed to fragment focus, fosters behaviors that, when multiplied across millions, alter the rhythms of work, communication, and decision-making on a societal level. Attention, once a private resource, has become a communal commodity, the depletion of which affects everything from productivity to governance. This transition is not merely a consequence of technological evolution but a reflection of broader shifts in values and priorities, where immediacy is rewarded, and depth is increasingly marginalized.

At the societal level, the aggregated effects of cognitive overload manifest in a diminished capacity for shared understanding and coordinated action. Public discourse fractures into disparate streams, each vying for attention, often through sensationalism rather than substance. Institutions, whether workplaces, governments, or media organizations, adapt to these dynamics by prioritizing immediacy over foresight, reactive measures over proactive planning. The result is a society that struggles to focus on its most pressing challenges, where the collective attention span mirrors the distracted state of its individuals. What emerges is not simply a loss of focus but a fundamental reconfiguration of how society processes information, engages in dialogue, and envisions its future.

This shift, though gradual and often imperceptible, raises profound questions about the sustainability of a culture that thrives on distraction.

THE PRODUCTIVITY PARADOX IN MODERN WORKPLACES

The promise of digital technologies in modern workplaces has always been one of increased efficiency, streamlined communication, and enhanced productivity. Yet, paradoxically, these same tools often undermine the very outcomes they claim to support. The productivity paradox lies in the friction between the affordances of technology and the ways they exploit human attentional vulnerabilities. Notifications, instant messaging platforms, and email chains fragment workflows, creating a state of perpetual partial attention. Workers are pulled in multiple directions, switching tasks rapidly, which not only reduces efficiency but also depletes cognitive resources. This phenomenon, often labeled as "context switching," hinders deep work—the sustained, focused effort required for complex problem-solving and innovation.

Beyond individual consequences, the productivity paradox has systemic implications for organizations. Metrics-driven cultures that value visible busyness over substantive outcomes exacerbate the problem, fostering environments where responsiveness is prized over thoughtfulness. Employees, conditioned to prioritize immediate replies and constant availability, find themselves in a cycle of reactive work that stifles creativity and long-term planning. The illusion of productivity perpetuated by digital engagement masks the erosion of meaningful contributions, as time spent on superficial tasks eclipses time devoted to strategic thinking. In this way, the tools intended to enhance workplace performance often entangle it in a web of inefficiency, creating an enduring paradox that challenges the foundations of modern work.

FRAGMENTATION OF PUBLIC DISCOURSE

The fragmentation of public discourse is one of the most profound societal consequences of a digitally-mediated attention economy. As platforms prioritize engagement above all else, the content that captures attention is often sensationalized, emotionally charged, or polarizing. Algorithms designed to maximize clicks and shares amplify divisive material, creating echo chambers where individuals are exposed primarily to perspectives that reinforce their existing beliefs. This selective exposure erodes the shared informational foundation necessary for constructive dialogue, replacing it with fractured narratives that deepen ideological divides.

The structure of online interaction further exacerbates this fragmentation. Nuanced discussions are often reduced to brief, oversimplified statements that fit the constraints of social media formats. Complex issues—ranging from climate change to public health policy—are distilled into slogans or headlines that obscure their intricacies, leaving little room for thoughtful deliberation. This environment fosters a climate where emotional reactivity trumps rational engagement, and the loudest voices often drown out more measured contributions.

Moreover, the decline of trust in traditional institutions and media, fueled in part by the proliferation of misinformation, compounds the issue. As individuals increasingly rely on digital platforms for news and social interaction, the line between fact and opinion blurs, leading to a contested reality in which consensus becomes elusive. This fragmentation undermines not only the quality of public discourse but also the ability to address collective challenges. A society incapable of sustained, collaborative attention risks stagnation, as the focus required to tackle long-term issues is continually diverted by the immediacy and noise of the digital sphere.

FRAGMENTATION OF PUBLIC DISCOURSE

The digital landscape has redefined how societies communicate, giving rise to profound fragmentation in public discourse. As platforms incentivize the production and consumption of content that triggers immediate engagement, the subtle, nuanced dialogue essential for democratic and collaborative problem-solving is eroded. The rise of algorithms engineered to prioritize virality and emotional resonance leads to a proliferation of sensationalized content, disproportionately amplifying extreme views while marginalizing moderate perspectives. This dynamic fosters ideological silos, where individuals are exposed primarily to information that aligns with their pre-existing beliefs, further deepening divisions across cultural, political, and social lines.

At the heart of this fragmentation lies the reduction of complex issues into consumable, attention-grabbing soundbites. Topics like climate change, public health crises, or economic reform are often oversimplified to fit the constraints of social media. Such brevity leaves little space for the nuanced analysis and comprehensive understanding required to address these multifaceted challenges. In this compressed environment, intellectual rigor and evidence-based reasoning give way to emotional reactivity, where popularity and immediacy overshadow accuracy and depth. The result is a public dialogue that increasingly rewards confrontation over collaboration and posturing over persuasion.

This fragmentation is further compounded by the destabilization of traditional sources of authority and credibility. In an era where misinformation spreads with the same speed as verified information, the once-clear delineation between fact and opinion has become blurred. Distrust in conventional media institutions has grown, as alternative narratives—often rooted in conspiracy theories or partisan agendas—find fertile ground online. This erosion of a shared informational baseline weakens society's ability to engage in collective decision-making, as individuals retreat into fragmented realities that rarely intersect.

The implications extend beyond ideological divides, influencing how societies mobilize around pressing global challenges. In a world where collective attention is fractured, the sustained focus required to address long-term issues is increasingly elusive. Efforts to confront existential threats such as climate change or systemic inequality are repeatedly undermined by the inability to foster unified priorities. The fragmentation of public discourse thus emerges not only as a symptom of digital distraction but as a significant barrier to societal progress, creating a cultural inertia that hinders meaningful action.

THE CULTURAL SHIFT TOWARD EPHEMERALITY

The digital age has ushered in a cultural shift toward ephemerality, profoundly altering how individuals and societies perceive and engage with information, relationships, and values. In a landscape where content is designed to be fleeting, with posts disappearing in hours or even minutes, the enduring weight of ideas has been replaced by the transient allure of immediacy. This focus on the ephemeral reflects a broader transformation in societal priorities, where permanence and depth are often sacrificed for the gratification of momentary relevance. The result is a collective consciousness increasingly oriented toward the now, detached from the continuum of historical understanding and forward-looking contemplation.

This shift has significant implications for how knowledge is shared and preserved. Traditional modes of cultural transmission relied on the longevity of written texts, oral histories, and established institutions to sustain collective memory. In contrast, digital platforms emphasize disposable content that thrives on novelty but quickly fades into obscurity. The ephemerality of this ecosystem discourages sustained intellectual engagement, as the rapid turnover of information overwhelms the capacity for critical reflection. When ideas are consumed in fragments and forgotten as quickly as they appear, the cumulative potential of knowledge-building diminishes, leaving individuals and communities unmoored from a sense of continuity and shared understanding.

Interpersonal relationships are not immune to this cultural drift. The design of digital interactions often prioritizes brevity and immediacy over depth and durability. Messages are crafted for the instant response, social bonds mediated by platforms that emphasize performative displays rather than substantive connection. This fosters a sense of impermanence not only in communication but in relationships themselves, as interactions are increasingly shaped by their utility in the present rather than their long-term significance. In this environment, emotional and social connections risk becoming transactional, their value dictated by the fleeting metrics of likes, views, and shares.

The cultural turn toward ephemerality also extends to how societies engage with broader issues and movements. Causes that gain traction online often enjoy an intense but short-lived spotlight, their momentum waning as new crises or trends emerge. This ephemeral activism, while capable of mobilizing rapid support, struggles to maintain the enduring focus necessary for systemic change. As public attention flits from one issue to another, the sustained efforts required to address complex challenges—whether social, environmental, or political—are undermined by the perpetual churn of the digital attention economy.

In this paradigm, the long-term consequences of prioritizing the ephemeral are profound. When permanence and intentionality are devalued, the foundational structures that sustain collective meaning and progress become destabilized. Societies risk losing their ability to anchor themselves in shared narratives, historical lessons, and enduring commitments, leaving them vulnerable to fragmentation and short-term thinking. While the appeal of ephemerality lies in its immediacy, the cultural costs of this shift demand critical reflection on how to reconcile the transient with the enduring in a world increasingly shaped by the fleeting.

SYSTEMS THINKING: FEEDBACK LOOPS AND AMPLIFICATION

The societal implications of cognitive overload cannot be fully understood without considering the systemic feedback loops that amplify its effects. Modern digital systems, particularly those governed by algorithmic processes, operate in ways that not only reflect but actively reinforce patterns of human behavior, creating cycles that escalate distraction and disengagement. These feedback loops are neither accidental nor benign; they emerge from the interplay between user behavior, platform design, and the overarching incentives of the attention economy, creating self-perpetuating systems that magnify both individual and collective vulnerabilities.

At the center of these systems lies the algorithmic drive to maximize engagement. Platforms are designed to track user behavior meticulously, identifying preferences, habits, and vulnerabilities to refine their ability to capture attention. This continuous optimization creates a cycle in which users are shown increasingly tailored content, reinforcing their existing behaviors and preferences. Over time, this can narrow the scope of attention and deepen reliance on instant gratification, eroding the capacity for sustained focus or critical engagement. The amplification of these tendencies is not merely a byproduct of technological efficiency but a direct consequence of systems designed to exploit them.

This dynamic becomes even more concerning when applied at scale. Individual patterns of attention and behavior are aggregated and analyzed, allowing platforms to predict and shape collective trends. The result is a form of emergent behavior in which societal attention coalesces around particular issues, narratives, or controversies, often driven more by virality and sensationalism than by substance or importance. The rapid oscillation between fleeting points of focus creates a societal echo chamber, where the amplification of specific themes comes at the cost of broader, more balanced discourse. In this context, the capacity for communities to address long-term challenges or engage in reflective dialogue is diminished, as the collective gaze is constantly redirected by the algorithms that mediate public attention.

Feedback loops also contribute to the reinforcement of systemic inequalities. As algorithms prioritize engagement, they often perpetuate biases inherent in the data they are trained on, magnifying disparities and entrenching existing power dynamics. Marginalized voices may struggle to gain visibility within these systems, as their content is less likely to align with the metrics of engagement that drive amplification. Similarly, issues requiring sustained attention—such as climate change or systemic injustice—are at a disadvantage in systems that prioritize immediacy and spectacle. The result is a feedback loop in which the structures of cognitive overload disproportionately affect those already at the margins, exacerbating societal divides.

The amplification of cognitive overload through systemic feedback loops is further compounded by the sheer scale of these networks. Unlike localized or isolated systems, digital platforms operate globally, with the potential to influence billions of users simultaneously. This global reach means that patterns of attention, distraction, and disengagement are not confined to individual communities or cultures but are woven into the fabric of a hyperconnected world. The cascading effects of these patterns can ripple across societies, affecting everything from political stability to cultural cohesion, as the amplification of short-term thinking undermines the ability to address shared, long-term challenges.

Recognizing the systemic nature of these feedback loops underscores the need for solutions that go beyond individual behavior or technological fixes. Addressing the amplification of cognitive overload requires a shift in how platforms are designed, regulated, and incentivized. It calls for an approach rooted in systems thinking, one that acknowledges the interconnectedness of individual actions, technological processes, and societal outcomes. Without such a perspective, efforts to mitigate cognitive overload risk being overwhelmed by the very systems they seek to change, leaving societies trapped in a cycle of escalating distraction and disengagement.

ETHICAL AND POLICY CONSIDERATIONS

The pervasive societal implications of cognitive overload, amplified through systemic feedback loops, demand an urgent ethical and policy-oriented response. The ethical considerations extend beyond individual autonomy and well-being, challenging us to rethink the frameworks that govern how technology is developed, deployed, and sustained in society. Addressing these challenges requires a reevaluation of the moral responsibilities of technology creators, the regulatory frameworks that oversee digital platforms, and the societal norms that shape our interaction with technology.

At the heart of the ethical dilemma lies the issue of consent and agency. Modern digital platforms operate in ways that often obscure their mechanisms of influence, leaving users unaware of how their behaviors are being monitored, analyzed, and manipulated. This lack of transparency erodes meaningful consent, as individuals cannot make fully informed choices about their engagement with technology. Ethical design, therefore, must prioritize clarity and honesty, ensuring that users understand how their attention is being commodified and the trade-offs involved in their digital interactions. Without this foundation, the relationship between users and platforms remains asymmetrical, favoring the interests of the latter at the expense of the former.

Another pressing ethical concern is the unequal distribution of harm caused by cognitive overload. Vulnerable populations, including children, adolescents, and those with preexisting mental health conditions, are disproportionately affected by the attention economy's exploitative practices. Children, for example, are particularly susceptible to the psychological mechanisms embedded in digital design, such as the lure of novelty and the compulsive draw of rewards. This raises questions about the moral obligations of platforms to protect their most vulnerable users and the societal responsibility to impose limits on practices that exploit developmental or psychological vulnerabilities for profit.

The societal costs of cognitive overload also call for a broader conversation about collective responsibility. The polarization of discourse, the erosion of public attention, and the amplification of inequities are not merely byproducts of technological innovation but the direct consequences of design choices that prioritize profit over societal well-being. Ethical considerations must address the moral imperatives of balancing innovation with the public good, recognizing that technology is never neutral but always shaped by human values and intentions. This requires a shift from a reactive to a proactive approach, where ethical foresight becomes integral to the development of digital systems.

Policy interventions play a critical role in addressing these ethical challenges, offering a pathway to systemic change. Regulatory frameworks must go beyond surface-level adjustments to address the root causes of cognitive overload. This includes enforcing transparency in algorithmic design, mandating disclosures about data usage and manipulation, and imposing restrictions on practices that exacerbate attentional harms. Policy initiatives must also focus on fostering digital literacy, equipping individuals and communities with the skills needed to navigate the complexities of the attention economy. Such measures can help mitigate the asymmetries of power between users and platforms, empowering individuals to reclaim agency over their digital lives.

International collaboration is essential in this context, as the global nature of digital platforms transcends national boundaries. Ethical standards and policy frameworks must be harmonized across jurisdictions to prevent regulatory arbitrage, where companies exploit discrepancies in national laws to avoid accountability. Furthermore, the establishment of global norms for humane technology design can serve as a counterbalance to the profit-driven imperatives that currently dominate the industry. These norms should prioritize values such as equity, sustainability, and human dignity, embedding them into the fabric of technological innovation.

Ultimately, addressing the ethical and policy dimensions of cognitive overload requires a paradigm shift in how society views technology. Rather than accepting the current trajectory as inevitable, we must recognize the agency we collectively hold to shape a digital future that aligns with our highest aspirations. This entails a commitment to accountability, not only for technology companies but also for policymakers, educators, and users themselves. By fostering a culture of ethical awareness and proactive regulation, we can begin to counteract the societal harms of cognitive overload and build systems that enhance, rather than diminish, the human capacity for focus, reflection, and meaningful engagement.

Part 3: Reclaiming Your Focus

The Mindful Technology User

Technology's influence on our daily lives operates with an almost imperceptible force, subtly shaping behaviors, thoughts, and emotions in ways that often go unnoticed. The design of digital platforms capitalizes on innate vulnerabilities within the human brain, exploiting evolutionary biases to keep users engaged. Infinite scroll, autoplay features, and algorithmically curated content are not merely conveniences; they are deliberate tools engineered to maximize attention capture. This manipulation is grounded in behavioral psychology, tapping into mechanisms such as intermittent reinforcement and the novelty-seeking tendencies of the brain. Each notification, like the chiming bell of a slot machine, delivers the promise of a reward—be it a social connection, a piece of information, or a fleeting sense of achievement. Over time, these stimuli create a dependency loop, conditioning users to respond reflexively and perpetuating cycles of distraction.

The profound implications of this dynamic lie in its subtlety. Unlike overt addictions, which are easily identifiable and stigmatized, technology addiction operates under the guise of utility and productivity. Social media platforms, streaming services, and even productivity apps present themselves as indispensable tools for modern life, their addictive qualities hidden behind layers of functionality. This duality makes it challenging for individuals to recognize when their engagement has crossed into compulsion. Moreover, the very architecture of these technologies is designed to erode self-regulation. Algorithms optimize for engagement metrics, constantly recalibrating to deliver precisely the type of content that will prolong user interaction. The result is a digital environment that constantly competes for cognitive resources, leaving individuals with little space to disengage and reflect.

Essentially, this relentless demand for attention is not neutral; it is a product of the attention economy, where human focus is commodified and sold to the highest bidder. This commodification has systemic implications, prioritizing engagement over well-being and fostering a culture where distraction becomes the norm. The unseen hand of technology ensures that individuals remain tethered to their devices, their interactions driven not by conscious choice but by the invisible scripts embedded within the digital systems they navigate. Recognizing this manipulation is the first step toward regaining autonomy, yet breaking free from such deeply ingrained habits requires more than awareness. It necessitates a fundamental shift in the way individuals interact with technology, as well as a broader cultural reckoning with the values that underpin the digital age.

Digital Decluttering: Reclaiming Space for Thought

In a world where digital noise constantly competes for attention, the act of decluttering one's technological environment is not merely an exercise in organization but a profound step toward reclaiming cognitive sovereignty. The human brain, designed to process information in manageable chunks, becomes overwhelmed when inundated with a relentless stream of notifications, messages, and alerts. Each competing stimulus imposes a cognitive toll, fragmenting attention and depleting mental resources. Digital decluttering offers a pathway to alleviate this burden, creating space for reflection, focus, and intentional engagement.

The process begins with an honest appraisal of one's digital habits, an often uncomfortable but necessary confrontation with the extent of technological entanglement. Apps, notifications, and digital tools, though originally intended to simplify life, frequently contribute to its complexity. Decluttering involves identifying and eliminating superfluous or redundant elements that siphon mental energy without providing meaningful value. It is an act of prioritization, of distinguishing between tools that serve personal or professional goals and those that merely exploit attention for their own ends.

A practical implementation might start with notifications, those persistent pings that hijack focus with trivial demands for immediate response. By turning off nonessential alerts, individuals can reclaim the rhythm of their day, reducing reactive behavior and fostering proactive thought. Similarly, auditing apps for relevance and utility can pare down digital environments to their functional core, replacing the clutter of unused or distracting applications with tools that genuinely enhance productivity or well-being. Such choices, though small, yield significant cumulative effects, easing the cognitive load and restoring a sense of control.

Decluttering, however, is not solely about reduction; it is also about intention. The act invites users to rethink their relationship with technology, to move from passive consumption to active engagement. Curating digital spaces to align with personal values and goals transforms these environments into extensions of individual agency rather than sources of external pressure. This reorientation fosters mindfulness, encouraging users to approach their digital interactions with deliberation rather than compulsion.

Ultimately, digital decluttering is an act of resistance against the pervasive forces of the attention economy. It reclaims cognitive bandwidth for pursuits that require sustained focus, such as creative endeavors, deep learning, and meaningful interpersonal connections. While the process requires effort and ongoing maintenance, its rewards are profound, offering a quieter, clearer mental space in which thought and intention can flourish. In a society driven by distraction, the deliberate act of simplifying one's digital world becomes a powerful assertion of autonomy.

NOTIFICATION MANAGEMENT: INTERRUPTING THE INTERRUPTIONS

In the cacophony of modern life, notifications serve as the ever-present interruptions that fracture attention and corrode focus. They exist as the technological embodiment of the world's demand for immediacy, diverting mental resources with every chime, buzz, or flashing icon. While notifications claim to enhance connectivity and efficiency, their unchecked presence often fosters a reactive rather than intentional state of mind, reducing the capacity for deep work and sustained thought. The art of notification management, therefore, becomes essential—not merely as a strategy for productivity but as a safeguard for mental clarity and cognitive health.

Effective notification management begins with understanding the psychological mechanisms that make these alerts so disruptive. Each notification operates as a trigger for a cognitive shift, pulling the mind from its current task and forcing an evaluative response. Even if dismissed without action, the mental residue of the interruption lingers, known as attentional residue, impairing the ability to return to the original focus with full concentration. This phenomenon compounds over time, leading to fragmented thinking, reduced productivity, and heightened stress levels.

To counteract this, individuals must critically assess which notifications truly demand their immediate attention. This involves a deliberate categorization of alerts, distinguishing between those essential to daily functioning—such as critical work updates or time-sensitive communications—and those designed merely to entice interaction, like social media prompts or promotional emails. Turning off nonessential notifications is a straightforward but powerful intervention, creating a more intentional flow of information into one's cognitive space.

Time-based notification batching presents another practical approach. Rather than allowing constant interruptions, individuals can set designated intervals to review messages or alerts, enabling them to engage with their digital tools on their own terms. This practice not only minimizes disruptions but also reinforces a sense of agency over technology use. Similarly, customizing notification settings across devices and applications allows users to further refine their digital experience, reducing the mental clutter associated with unnecessary alerts.

The benefits of such strategies extend beyond the immediate reduction of interruptions. By managing notifications effectively, individuals can cultivate an environment conducive to deeper engagement and sustained focus. This, in turn, fosters greater emotional resilience, as the constant sense of urgency imposed by relentless alerts dissipates, allowing for a more measured and reflective pace of interaction with both technology and the wider world.

Ultimately, notification management is not about severing ties with the digital realm but about reshaping one's relationship with it. It transforms technology from a source of incessant demand into a tool of deliberate utility. In mastering the interruptions, individuals reclaim the capacity to think, create, and connect without the perpetual distraction of a world vying for their attention.

The Art of Mindful Technology Use

The art of mindful technology use lies at the intersection of intentionality and awareness, a deliberate effort to redefine one's engagement with digital tools in a way that aligns with personal values and mental well-being. Unlike reactive patterns of interaction, where technology dictates attention through its constant stream of demands, mindful usage requires a proactive approach: one in which the user, rather than the device, governs the relationship. This shift is not merely a behavioral adjustment but a cognitive and emotional recalibration, fostering a healthier balance between the digital and the real.

At its core, mindful technology use begins with presence—the ability to remain fully engaged with the task or moment at hand without succumbing to the seductive pull of digital distractions. This practice often involves a heightened awareness of one's habits, such as the unconscious compulsion to check a smartphone during moments of idleness or the habitual opening of social media apps during work breaks. By bringing these behaviors into conscious focus, individuals can begin to identify triggers and patterns that perpetuate mindless scrolling or multitasking.

Central to this approach is the practice of setting boundaries, both temporal and spatial. Temporal boundaries involve creating specific windows of time for technology use, such as designated periods for checking emails or scrolling through newsfeeds, while committing to screen-free intervals for activities like meals, conversations, or relaxation. Spatial boundaries, on the other hand, involve redefining the physical relationship with technology—for instance, keeping devices out of the bedroom to protect the sanctity of sleep or establishing tech-free zones within the home to encourage meaningful face-to-face interactions. These boundaries serve as tangible reminders of the distinction between digital engagement and personal presence.

Mindfulness in technology use also requires a reorientation of purpose. Instead of approaching devices with the vague intention of "seeing what's new," individuals can adopt a goal-oriented mindset, engaging with technology only when it serves a specific, predefined purpose. This practice not only reduces the likelihood of becoming ensnared in endless cycles of distraction but also enhances the quality of interaction with digital content, as intentional use fosters greater focus and satisfaction.

Equally important is the cultivation of self-compassion within this framework. Given the addictive design of many digital platforms, lapses into mindless use are almost inevitable. Rather than viewing such moments as failures, a mindful approach encourages individuals to acknowledge them without judgment and to gently refocus their attention. This perspective reinforces a growth mindset, emphasizing progress over perfection in the journey toward healthier digital habits.

The art of mindful technology use ultimately transforms devices from agents of distraction into tools for empowerment. By fostering intentionality, boundaries, and self-awareness, individuals can reclaim their time, focus, and emotional equilibrium, navigating the digital age with greater clarity and purpose. In doing so, they not only protect their cognitive and mental health but also create space for the deeper connections and reflections that define a life well-lived.

PRACTICAL TOOLS AND TECHNIQUES FOR DIGITAL WELL-BEING

Practical tools and techniques for digital well-being provide the scaffolding necessary to translate mindful intentions into actionable behaviors, empowering individuals to regain control over their digital lives. These tools are not merely theoretical abstractions but tangible strategies that address the intricate challenges posed by an always-connected world. By integrating these methods into daily routines, individuals can construct a sustainable framework for digital engagement that prioritizes focus, mental clarity, and personal fulfillment.

One cornerstone technique is the use of scheduling to regulate digital engagement. By allocating specific blocks of time for activities such as checking emails, browsing social media, or responding to messages, individuals can confine their technology use within intentional boundaries, avoiding the cognitive fatigue of constant accessibility. Complementing this strategy is the implementation of designated "offline hours," during which all devices are silenced or powered down to facilitate uninterrupted work, relaxation, or sleep. Such scheduling fosters a rhythm that balances connectivity with disconnection, mitigating the cumulative strain of incessant digital demands.

Another transformative tool is the strategic curation of digital environments. This involves decluttering devices by uninstalling redundant apps, disabling non-essential notifications, and organizing interfaces to minimize distractions. For example, relocating productivity tools to the home screen while relegating entertainment apps to less accessible locations can subtly redirect habits toward more purposeful interactions. Similarly, browser extensions and apps designed to block distracting websites or monitor screen time provide invaluable support, serving as digital guardrails that reinforce intentionality.

Mindful engagement with technology also benefits from the integration of reflective practices. Journaling about daily technology use—cataloging the amount of time spent on specific apps, the emotions associated with this use, and the alignment of activities with personal goals—can illuminate patterns and prompt necessary adjustments. Over time, this practice fosters a deeper awareness of the ways in which technology shapes cognition, mood, and productivity, enabling users to recalibrate their habits with greater precision.

Equally important is the cultivation of "micro-disconnects," brief intervals during which individuals step away from devices to reconnect with their immediate environment. These moments, whether spent in nature, engaging in physical activity, or practicing mindfulness meditation, serve as antidotes to the overstimulation of constant connectivity. By incorporating such pauses into their routines, individuals can refresh their cognitive resources and recalibrate their attention, enhancing both productivity and emotional well-being.

Perhaps the most impactful technique for digital well-being lies in fostering a communal ethos of mindful technology use. When families, workplaces, or social groups adopt shared guidelines—such as tech-free dinners, digital detox weekends, or collective accountability for screen time—individuals benefit from a supportive environment that normalizes intentional disconnection. These collective efforts not only amplify individual resolve but also create a cultural shift that values presence and attentiveness over the illusion of perpetual availability.

Through the adoption of practical tools and techniques, digital well-being becomes an achievable reality rather than an aspirational ideal. By anchoring these practices in intentionality and reflection, individuals can navigate the digital age with resilience and agency, transforming their relationship with technology into one of empowerment rather than entrapment.

SUSTAINING LONG-TERM CHANGE

Sustaining long-term change in the realm of digital well-being transcends the adoption of isolated strategies, requiring a deliberate cultivation of habits that reinforce mindfulness and balance over time. The challenge lies not merely in making initial adjustments but in embedding these shifts into the fabric of everyday life, ensuring they endure in the face of evolving technologies and external pressures. This process demands a combination of self-awareness, adaptability, and a commitment to aligning digital practices with deeper personal values.

At the core of lasting change is the recognition that digital habits are rarely static; they are dynamic, shaped by both internal needs and external stimuli. To sustain progress, individuals must periodically reflect on their relationship with technology, assessing whether their current practices continue to serve their goals. This reflective process can be guided by questions such as: *Is my technology use enhancing or detracting from my well-being? Have I inadvertently reverted to behaviors I sought to change?* By regularly revisiting these inquiries, individuals can identify early signs of slippage and course-correct before patterns become entrenched.

Central to this sustained effort is the development of what might be termed a "digital philosophy," a personalized framework of principles that guide one's engagement with technology. Such a philosophy might emphasize priorities like intentionality, presence, and the preservation of mental clarity, providing a touchstone against which decisions about digital use can be evaluated. For instance, a guiding principle might be, *I will engage with technology in ways that amplify my focus and creativity while limiting distraction.* This philosophical grounding transforms technology use from a reactive habit into a deliberate practice, tethered to a sense of purpose.

Equally critical is the creation of supportive structures that reduce reliance on sheer willpower. Automation tools, such as scheduled "do not disturb" settings or app usage caps, alleviate the cognitive load of constantly policing oneself. Similarly, environmental cues—like keeping devices out of bedrooms or designating specific spaces for screen use—serve as physical reminders to uphold healthy boundaries. By externalizing some of the effort required to maintain change, these structures make it easier to adhere to new habits over the long term.

Another powerful mechanism for sustaining digital well-being is the establishment of rituals that celebrate intentional disconnection. These might include weekly technology-free sabbaths, evening routines centered around offline activities, or annual "digital detoxes" that serve as a symbolic reset. Such rituals provide both structure and symbolic weight, reinforcing the notion that stepping away from screens is not a deprivation but a meaningful act of self-care and renewal. Over time, these practices can shift perceptions of disconnection from a momentary reprieve to an integral part of a balanced life.

Community engagement also plays an essential role in fostering lasting change. Whether through family agreements, workplace initiatives, or broader social movements advocating for ethical tech use, collective efforts create an environment in which digital mindfulness is normalized and supported. By participating in a community that shares similar goals, individuals benefit from shared accountability and the inspiration that comes from witnessing others navigate similar challenges. These networks of support provide resilience against moments of doubt or backsliding, anchoring individual efforts in a larger cultural context.

Ultimately, the sustainability of digital well-being hinges on a willingness to adapt as circumstances change. Technologies will continue to evolve, and with them, the demands they place on attention and cognition. Sustaining progress requires a mindset of continuous learning and experimentation, an openness to revising strategies as new challenges and opportunities arise. By embracing this iterative approach, individuals can ensure that their relationship with technology remains a source of empowerment, aligned with their aspirations and resilient to the forces of the attention economy. Through persistence, reflection, and intentionality, the journey toward digital well-being becomes not just a momentary adjustment but a lifelong practice.

A Vision of Empowered Tech Use

A vision of empowered tech use begins with redefining the relationship between humanity and its digital tools. Rather than serving as passive consumers in a system designed to monopolize attention, individuals can reclaim agency by transforming technology into an ally that aligns with personal values and aspirations. Empowerment in this context is not about abstinence from technology but about mastery—leveraging its strengths while mitigating its potential to disrupt, distract, or dominate.

At the heart of this vision is the principle of intentionality, the conscious act of deciding how and why technology is used. This requires individuals to take stock of their digital habits, distinguishing between interactions that enhance their lives and those that detract from their goals. Empowered tech use is guided by clarity of purpose: whether it is using a productivity app to streamline workflows, engaging with social media to deepen genuine connections, or curating a news feed to stay informed without succumbing to anxiety-inducing overload. When technology is wielded with deliberate intention, it ceases to control and instead becomes a means of amplifying human potential.

An empowered approach also embraces adaptability, recognizing that the landscape of technology is in constant flux. Just as tools evolve, so too must the strategies for integrating them into daily life. This requires cultivating a mindset of critical engagement—one that questions default settings, evaluates the motives behind algorithmic designs, and resists the allure of trends that prioritize profit over well-being. By remaining agile and discerning, individuals can navigate technological change without losing sight of their own needs and priorities.

A cornerstone of this vision is the democratization of digital literacy, empowering people to understand and critically engage with the forces shaping their online experiences. Education plays a pivotal role here, equipping users with the skills to decipher manipulative designs, protect their privacy, and make informed choices about the platforms they engage with. Empowerment emerges when individuals no longer feel at the mercy of opaque systems but instead possess the knowledge to navigate them confidently and assertively.

Central to the empowered user is the cultivation of balance—a harmonious coexistence with technology that preserves space for offline experiences, deep relationships, and introspection. This balance is not achieved through rigid rules or blanket avoidance but through a nuanced understanding of when and how to step away. Empowered users set boundaries that honor their need for focus and rest, recognizing that these moments of disconnection enhance their ability to engage meaningfully both online and off.

Empowered tech use is also a collective endeavor, extending beyond individual choices to demand systemic change. Advocacy for ethical technology design, transparency in data use, and accountability from tech companies ensures that digital environments foster well-being rather than exploitation. In this vision, empowerment is not limited to personal agency but encompasses the shared responsibility to shape a technological ecosystem that supports collective flourishing.

Ultimately, empowered tech use is not an end state but a continuous practice, a dynamic relationship that evolves with the individual and their circumstances. It is about transforming technology from a source of overwhelm into a tool for meaningful engagement, creativity, and connection. By embracing this vision, individuals are not only reclaiming their focus but also contributing to a broader cultural shift—one that values attention as a precious resource and prioritizes human well-being over technological consumption. In doing so, they lay the foundation for a future where technology serves as a partner in human growth rather than a barrier to it.

Cultivating Attention and Focus

Imagine sitting down to focus on an important task, one that requires your full attention and creativity. The cursor blinks on a blank screen, waiting for you to begin, but before typing a single word, your phone buzzes. A notification flashes—a quick reply seems harmless. Moments later, you're scrolling through social media, lost in a flood of updates, advertisements, and viral videos. The task remains untouched, the mental energy you reserved for it dissipating with every flick of your thumb. This scenario, all too familiar, is emblematic of the battle for our attention in the modern world.

We are bombarded by stimuli at every turn, from the incessant ping of notifications to the alluring promise of infinite content. Each demand on our attention fragments it further, leaving us juggling countless threads of thought without ever weaving them into something meaningful. The result is a growing inability to concentrate for extended periods, to engage deeply with ideas, or even to sit quietly with our own thoughts. What feels like a momentary distraction is, in reality, part of a broader assault on our cognitive resources—an erosion of focus that leaves us drained, anxious, and unfulfilled.

This fragmentation comes at a cost far greater than missed deadlines or incomplete tasks. It undermines our ability to connect with others, to pursue creative endeavors, and to cultivate a sense of purpose. When our days are defined by constant interruption, our lives begin to feel shallow and scattered, as though we are skimming the surface of existence without ever plunging into its depths. Attention, once a tool we wield to shape our world, has become a resource we scarcely control, siphoned away by forces far beyond our immediate awareness.

If this loss feels inevitable, it's because the systems around us are designed to make it so. The platforms we use, the devices we carry, and even the cultural norms we adopt all reinforce the expectation that we should always be available, always connected, always consuming. Yet, while these forces shape our behavior, they do not determine it. The battle for attention, though formidable, is not unwinnable. Like any skill, focus can be nurtured, strengthened, and reclaimed.

This chapter marks the beginning of that reclamation. The first step is recognizing the patterns that ensnare us, the second is committing to change, and the third is embracing practices that can help rebuild the cognitive foundations we've lost. It is not an easy path—distraction is seductive, and focus demands effort. But in an age of perpetual distraction, cultivating attention is a radical act of self-empowerment, a way of reclaiming not just what we do but who we are.

TRAINING ATTENTION AS A SKILL

If attention is the currency of the digital age, then most of us have been spending it recklessly, leaving our reserves depleted. Yet, despite the pervasive sense of helplessness that cognitive overload creates, there is a profound truth that offers hope: attention is not fixed or finite. It is a skill—one that can be cultivated, sharpened, and strengthened with deliberate effort. Much like physical fitness, where consistent training transforms muscles and stamina, the mind's capacity to focus improves when given the right exercises and conditions.

This idea—that attention is a trainable skill—marks a critical shift in how we view ourselves in relation to the forces that dominate modern life. Distraction, while omnipresent, is not insurmountable; it is the product of habits, environments, and systems that can be adjusted or resisted. With intentional practice, the very same brain that has adapted to the quick fixes of dopamine-driven scrolling can adapt to deeper, more sustained engagement. Neuroscience has shown us that the brain's plasticity, its ability to rewire itself in response to repeated behaviors, offers a pathway to reclaim control over our attention.

This reframing transforms attention from a passive experience to an active discipline. It suggests that focus is not something we either have or lack but something we can build, like a craftsman refining their tools or an athlete honing their form. It means that the scattered, overstimulated state so many of us inhabit is not a life sentence but a challenge to overcome. The battle for attention, once seen through this lens, is not a losing fight against technology but an opportunity to rediscover the power of intention in shaping how we think, feel, and act.

Training attention, then, becomes not just a necessity but an act of self-respect and resistance. It is a refusal to let external forces dictate the rhythm of our minds. And just as with any skill, the journey begins with small, deliberate steps—simple exercises that, over time, build into habits capable of restoring clarity and focus. With commitment, the scattered mind can become centered, and the fractured self can find cohesion. The practices that follow are not about perfection or isolation but about reclaiming the freedom to direct your attention toward what truly matters.

PRACTICAL STRATEGIES FOR STRENGTHENING FOCUS

Reclaiming attention begins with actionable steps—practices that anchor the mind and rebuild its capacity for focus. These strategies are not quick fixes or one-size-fits-all solutions; they require patience and persistence, offering gradual but lasting change. At their core is the understanding that the mind, like the body, thrives on consistent and intentional effort. The following exercises serve as a foundation, equipping us to resist distraction and cultivate deeper engagement with the world around us.

Meditation is one of the most powerful tools in this journey. Far from being an abstract or esoteric practice, meditation is a structured way of training the mind to observe and redirect its wandering impulses. At its simplest, it involves sitting quietly, focusing on the breath, and bringing attention back whenever it drifts. This act of returning—again and again—is where the transformation lies. Over time, it strengthens the prefrontal cortex, the part of the brain responsible for concentration and decision-making, and quiets the noise of the limbic system, where reactivity and distraction originate. Even a few minutes a day can sharpen focus, reduce anxiety, and create a sense of mental spaciousness.

Alongside meditation is the practice of deep work, the deliberate effort to concentrate on cognitively demanding tasks without interruption. In a world that values multitasking, deep work may feel countercultural, even uncomfortable. Yet its benefits are profound. By dedicating blocks of uninterrupted time to a single task—free from the pull of notifications or the temptation of quick diversions—we tap into a state of flow, where focus becomes effortless and creativity thrives. Creating these conditions requires intentional boundaries: turning off devices, informing colleagues or family of the need for quiet, and structuring the environment to support immersion. Deep work is not merely productive; it is fulfilling, a reminder of the satisfaction that comes from sustained engagement.

Intentional breaks from screens are equally essential. The modern mind is overstimulated, inundated with pixels and pings that demand constant attention. Stepping away restores balance, allowing the brain to recover from the fatigue of overuse. This is not about disengagement but about creating space for different kinds of stimulation—natural, physical, or creative. A walk in the park, a few minutes tending to plants, or even staring out of a window can reset the mind. These moments of pause, though simple, act as antidotes to the hyperactive pace of modern life, replenishing attention and fostering a renewed sense of clarity.

Equally important is learning to embrace monotasking, the practice of doing one thing at a time with full presence. Multitasking, often glorified as a marker of efficiency, scatters attention and diminishes the quality of our efforts. Monotasking, in contrast, anchors the mind, allowing it to fully process and engage with what is at hand. This can begin with small acts: savoring a meal without scrolling on a phone, listening intently to a conversation without formulating a response, or reading a book without glancing at notifications. These moments may seem insignificant, but they are foundational to reestablishing the habit of sustained focus.

Taken together, these strategies form a toolkit for rebuilding the attention we have lost. They are not about rejecting technology or retreating from the modern world but about forging a healthier relationship with it. Each practice is a step toward reclaiming agency, a way of telling the world that your attention is yours to direct. Strengthening focus is not an overnight transformation, nor is it linear. It requires experimentation, adaptation, and, above all, commitment. Yet with each small step, the scattered mind becomes steadier, and the fractured self begins to feel whole again.

REAL-WORLD APPLICATIONS

The power of focus is not an abstract concept but a reality demonstrated through countless stories of individuals who have mastered their attention amidst distraction. These real-world applications and anecdotes serve as both inspiration and proof that the battle for attention can be won. They show us not only what is possible but how others have navigated the same challenges we face today.

Consider the life of Carl Jung, one of the most influential psychologists of the 20th century, who retreated to a stone tower in the Swiss countryside to escape the distractions of his time and focus on his groundbreaking work. The tower, devoid of electricity or running water, became a sanctuary for deep thinking, a place where Jung could write, reflect, and wrestle with his ideas without interruption. Jung's example reminds us that focus often requires deliberate environmental choices, an active removal of distractions to make space for what truly matters.

In the modern era, many creatives and professionals have adopted similar practices to protect their attention. Writers like J.K. Rowling have spoken of retreating to quiet, secluded spaces to finish their work, free from the demands of daily life. Tech entrepreneur Jack Dorsey has shared how he incorporates mindfulness and daily meditation into his routine to manage the relentless pace of his industry. These stories show that even in the most demanding environments, individuals can reclaim their focus through intentional habits and environments designed to foster concentration.

On a more relatable scale, there is the story of a software engineer who struggled with the constant pull of notifications while working on a complex coding project. Recognizing the impact on his productivity, he committed to two hours of deep work every morning before checking his phone or email. The results were transformative: not only did his efficiency improve, but he also found a renewed sense of satisfaction in his work. This anecdote illustrates that reclaiming focus does not require a complete overhaul of life but small, deliberate adjustments to daily habits.

Equally powerful are the stories of those who have used focus to rebuild their personal lives. A young mother, overwhelmed by the demands of parenting and work, began incorporating intentional breaks into her day—pausing for five minutes to breathe deeply or take a walk outdoors. These moments of presence allowed her to reconnect with herself and her family, showing how focus can enrich not only professional achievements but personal relationships as well.

These narratives remind us that the practices of cultivating focus are not merely theoretical. They are grounded in the lived experiences of people who have faced similar struggles and found ways to thrive. Their stories act as guideposts, illuminating a path forward for anyone seeking to reclaim their attention in a distracted world. By interweaving these real-world applications with the practical strategies discussed earlier, we see not just how to cultivate focus but why it matters—and how profoundly it can transform the way we live and work.

The Deep Connection Between Habits and Identity

At the heart of cultivating focus lies a truth that extends beyond mere behavior: the habits we adopt are reflections of who we are and, more importantly, who we aspire to be. The link between habits and identity is profound. Every small, intentional act we take toward reclaiming our attention is a statement about the kind of person we are becoming. This connection transforms the process of building focus from a series of mechanical exercises into a deeply personal journey of self-discovery and transformation.

When you decide to set aside time for deep work, to silence notifications, or to meditate for even a few minutes each day, you are not simply adopting a new practice. You are reinforcing a narrative about yourself—a belief that you are someone capable of resisting distraction and embracing intention. These actions, small as they may seem, begin to reshape how you see yourself. A single choice to monotask rather than multitask becomes more than a momentary decision; it is a vote for a focused, deliberate life. Over time, these choices accumulate, solidifying an identity rooted in clarity, purpose, and self-control.

Consider someone who starts with a simple habit: dedicating the first 15 minutes of their morning to a quiet moment of reflection rather than reaching for their phone. At first, it feels unnatural, even inconvenient, but as the habit takes root, it becomes more than an act—it becomes part of who they are. They begin to see themselves as someone who values mindfulness over chaos, presence over immediacy. This shift in identity doesn't just make the habit easier to maintain; it makes it integral to their sense of self.

The reverse is also true. When our habits are dictated by distraction—endless scrolling, constant multitasking, or reacting to every notification—we begin to see ourselves as fragmented, scattered, or even powerless. These behaviors reinforce an identity of disconnection, making it harder to break free from the cycles of distraction. To reclaim our focus, we must consciously shift this narrative, aligning our actions with the person we wish to become.

The link between habits and identity also explains why sustainable change often feels gradual. We cannot transform overnight because identity is not built on a single choice but on the repeated confirmation of who we are through action. This is why small, consistent habits—meditation, deep work, screen breaks—are so powerful. Each one acts as a cornerstone, laying the foundation for a broader transformation in how we see ourselves and engage with the world.

As you adopt these habits, consider not just what you are doing but who you are becoming. Every time you choose focus over distraction, you are reinforcing an identity of intentionality. Every time you protect your attention from the pull of digital noise, you affirm your autonomy and strength. This journey is not about perfection but progress, a gradual but profound shift toward a life defined by clarity, purpose, and the freedom to direct your mind where it matters most.

An Invitation to Experiment

The journey to reclaim focus is not a rigid prescription but an open exploration, a chance to rediscover your capacity to direct your attention with intention. It's not about perfect adherence to routines or flawlessly avoiding distraction—it's about curiosity, persistence, and a willingness to try. This chapter has offered tools and practices, but their power lies not in the words on these pages but in your willingness to take them into your life and make them your own.

Think of this as an experiment, one where you are both the subject and the scientist. Begin with a single practice that resonates—a brief moment of meditation, a morning free from screens, or a dedicated hour of deep work. Observe how it feels, how it shapes your day, and how it shifts your perception of what is possible. Some methods will feel natural, others will challenge you, but every attempt is a step forward. Each success, no matter how small, is a glimpse of what focus can bring to your life: clarity, creativity, connection.

Be patient with yourself. This is not a race but a process of unfolding, of rediscovering skills that modern life has dulled. There will be moments of struggle, times when distraction feels insurmountable, but these are part of the journey. The key is not perfection but persistence—returning to the practice, adjusting where necessary, and allowing the effort to shape you over time.

As you experiment, allow room for discovery. You may find that certain practices resonate in unexpected ways or that your relationship with technology begins to shift in subtle but meaningful directions. You may notice a deepening sense of presence in your interactions, a newfound patience with yourself and others, or a rekindled curiosity about the world. These are signs that the experiment is working, that you are beginning to reclaim the agency that distraction has taken.

This is your invitation: to step away from the noise, to reclaim your attention, and to explore what focus can bring to your life. Treat this as an adventure, a way to reconnect with the person you are beneath the layers of distraction. You have everything you need to begin—the tools, the time, the ability. All that remains is the decision to start. In this act of experimentation, you are not just learning to focus; you are reclaiming a deeper sense of who you are and what you can achieve.

The Multitasking Myth

The world has long celebrated multitasking as the hallmark of efficiency, a badge of honor worn by those who claim to juggle tasks seamlessly. It has become a cultural ideal, reinforced by the constant hum of modern life that demands more, faster, and all at once. Yet, beneath this façade of productivity lies a deeply flawed premise. Multitasking, far from being a skill to admire, is a cognitive trap that fragments our attention, diminishes our focus, and leaves us drained and unfulfilled.

Research in cognitive neuroscience has repeatedly shown that the brain is not designed to focus on multiple tasks simultaneously. What we often call multitasking is, in fact, rapid task-switching—a process that forces the brain to constantly recalibrate its focus. This switching comes at a cost: slower progress, more errors, and a superficial engagement with whatever we are trying to do. Instead of excelling, we scatter our cognitive resources, stretching them too thin to be truly effective.

Nowhere is this problem more evident than in our relationship with technology. Smartphones, emails, and social media platforms bombard us with an endless stream of stimuli, each one vying for a slice of our attention. The digital age, in its quest for connectivity and convenience, has woven multitasking into the fabric of our daily lives. Answering an email while attending a meeting, scrolling through notifications while having a conversation, or splitting time between countless open browser tabs has become second nature. Yet, with each fractured moment, we sacrifice not just productivity but the depth and quality of our experience.

The illusion of productivity that multitasking offers is seductive but ultimately hollow. While we may feel busy, even accomplished, the truth is that divided attention prevents us from immersing ourselves fully in any single activity. It robs us of the opportunity to engage deeply, to think critically, and to create something meaningful. And the costs are not limited to our work; our personal lives suffer as well. How often do we listen half-heartedly, missing the nuance of a conversation because our minds are elsewhere? How frequently do we find ourselves distracted, unable to be truly present with the people we care about?

The problem lies not just in the act of multitasking itself but in the broader cultural narrative that equates busyness with success. The modern world has conditioned us to believe that doing more is inherently better, but in truth, this relentless pace is eroding our capacity for focus, creativity, and connection. Recognizing this myth is the first step toward reclaiming our attention and challenging the systems that perpetuate it.

THE CASE FOR MONOTASKING

If multitasking represents the myth of modern productivity, monotasking stands as its quiet counterpoint: a practice rooted in simplicity, intentionality, and the understanding that depth matters more than breadth. At its core, monotasking is the art of giving your full, undivided attention to one task at a time. This is not merely a rejection of multitasking but a reorientation—a deliberate choice to prioritize focus over fragmentation and depth over distraction.

The case for monotasking begins with the brain itself. Neurologically, we are wired to focus deeply on one thing at a time. When we direct all our cognitive resources to a single task, we enter a state of flow—a mental zone where time seems to dissolve, creativity flourishes, and productivity reaches its peak. In this state, the brain operates with remarkable efficiency, free from the constant recalibration required by task-switching. What emerges is not just faster work but better work: ideas are sharper, solutions are more innovative, and the satisfaction of completing a task feels tangible and rewarding.

Monotasking also fosters a sense of presence that is increasingly rare in a world dominated by distraction. When we commit to a single activity, whether it's writing, problem-solving, or even a conversation, we engage more deeply with it. This depth allows us to notice subtleties and connections that would otherwise be lost in the noise of competing demands. It's the difference between skimming the surface and diving into the depths, between a shallow glance and a meaningful gaze.

This practice extends beyond work and into the rhythms of daily life. Consider the act of having a meal without checking your phone or walking through a park without headphones. These moments, seemingly mundane, take on a richness when approached with full attention. You notice the texture of a dish, the pattern of sunlight through the trees, the nuances of your own thoughts. Monotasking invites us to savor life rather than rushing through it, reminding us that presence is as much about the small moments as it is the grand ones.

Critics may argue that monotasking feels impractical in a world that demands so much from us. Yet, the truth is that monotasking doesn't reduce what we accomplish—it transforms how we accomplish it. It forces us to prioritize, to focus on what truly matters rather than attempting to do everything at once. By giving undivided attention to a single task, we complete it more effectively and often in less time, freeing us to move on to the next with the same clarity and intent.

The case for monotasking is ultimately a case for reclaiming agency over how we use our time and energy. It's a refusal to allow the demands of the modern world to dictate the pace and quality of our lives. In choosing monotasking, we choose depth over shallowness, presence over distraction, and meaning over mere activity. It is, at its heart, a commitment to living deliberately.

DEFINING BOUNDARIES: WHY THEY MATTER

In a world that never truly powers down, where work bleeds into leisure and leisure is interrupted by the endless hum of notifications, boundaries are no longer a luxury—they are a necessity. Defining clear limits around how we use technology and allocate our attention is not an act of deprivation but of preservation. It is how we protect the most finite resource we have: our focus.

Boundaries matter because attention, once spent, cannot be reclaimed. Every moment given to a buzzing phone or a distracting app is a moment taken from something else: a project that demands your best thinking, a conversation that could deepen a relationship, or a quiet moment to simply be. Without boundaries, our days become a patchwork of interruptions, leaving little room for the sustained, meaningful engagement that makes life fulfilling.

The psychological toll of boundaryless living is immense. The absence of limits fosters decision fatigue—the mental exhaustion that comes from constantly evaluating whether to respond to a notification, check an app, or keep scrolling. It creates a sense of perpetual availability, where we feel compelled to respond instantly to every ping and email, even at the expense of our well-being. Over time, this erodes not only our focus but also our sense of autonomy. When we fail to set boundaries, we hand over control of our time and attention to external forces, leaving us reactive rather than intentional.

Defining boundaries around technology is, therefore, an act of reclaiming agency. It's about deciding, with clarity and conviction, where your attention will go—and where it will not. This might mean setting specific times for checking email or turning off notifications during meals and conversations. It might involve designating certain spaces, like the bedroom or the dining table, as device-free zones. These boundaries may feel small, even inconsequential, at first, but their impact is profound. They create pockets of focus and presence in an otherwise fragmented world, allowing us to engage deeply with what truly matters.

Boundaries also teach us, and those around us, to respect attention as a finite resource. When you establish limits—whether by silencing your phone during a creative session or letting colleagues know you won't respond to emails after hours—you send a clear message: attention is valuable, and it deserves protection. These small acts of self-respect can ripple outward, encouraging others to reevaluate their own habits and fostering a culture where focus is valued over constant availability.

At their core, boundaries are not restrictive; they are freeing. They carve out the mental and emotional space we need to think clearly, work effectively, and connect authentically. They remind us that we are not at the mercy of our devices or the demands of the modern world. With boundaries in place, we can reclaim our attention—not just for productivity but for the richer, more intentional lives that come when we decide what deserves our focus and what does not.

STRATEGIES FOR MONOTASKING AND BOUNDARY-SETTING

If understanding the importance of monotasking and boundaries is the first step, implementing them requires practical strategies that integrate seamlessly into daily life. Monotasking and boundary-setting are not innate skills but practices that can be cultivated with intention and consistency. The challenge lies not only in adopting these habits but in maintaining them amidst the relentless demands of the digital age.

Monotasking begins with a commitment to focus deeply on one task at a time, and this requires preparation. A productive monotasking session starts with clearing the mental and physical clutter that invites distraction. This might mean silencing your phone, closing unnecessary browser tabs, or simply tidying your workspace. By removing the triggers that tempt your attention, you create an environment conducive to focus. From here, it's about choosing a single task to immerse yourself in, setting a clear intention for what you aim to achieve, and giving it your full, undivided attention.

A particularly effective tool for monotasking is time-blocking, where specific periods are allocated to focused work. During these blocks, interruptions are minimized, and attention is directed solely toward the task at hand. Techniques like the Pomodoro method, which alternates intervals of concentrated work with short breaks, can help sustain focus while preventing burnout. These structured sessions allow you to approach tasks methodically, breaking them down into manageable portions while ensuring that each gets the attention it deserves.

Boundary-setting, on the other hand, is about creating guardrails that protect your time and attention from the constant encroachment of technology. A powerful strategy here is to establish digital curfews—set times in the day when screens are put away, whether it's an hour before bed or during meals with loved ones. These breaks from technology not only preserve focus but also nurture presence, allowing you to reconnect with the people and experiences around you.

Another approach is to use technology itself to enforce boundaries. Many devices now offer features like "Do Not Disturb," focus modes, or app limits, which can help you control when and how you interact with digital distractions. Setting specific times to check emails or social media, rather than allowing these activities to punctuate your day, can transform how you engage with technology. By limiting these interactions to designated windows, you regain control over your attention instead of reacting to every notification.

It's also important to communicate your boundaries to others. If you're dedicating a block of time to deep work, let colleagues or family members know that you won't be available during that period. Setting these expectations not only reinforces your commitment to focus but also encourages a culture of respect for attention and productivity.

Finally, monotasking and boundary-setting require self-awareness and adaptability. There will be days when distractions win and boundaries falter, but these moments are opportunities to reflect and recalibrate. The goal is not perfection but progress—a gradual reshaping of habits that prioritizes depth, presence, and intentionality. Over time, these practices become second nature, fostering a life where attention is directed with purpose and energy is spent on what truly matters.

A Vision for a Balanced Relationship with Technology

The goal is not to vilify technology or to retreat from its undeniable benefits, but to redefine our relationship with it—to find a balance that honors both its utility and our humanity. Technology, when wielded thoughtfully, has the potential to enhance our lives, fostering connections, enabling creativity, and solving problems that once seemed insurmountable. Yet, when it operates unchecked, it can just as easily fragment our attention, erode our well-being, and distance us from the very lives we are trying to enrich.

A balanced relationship with technology begins with the recognition that it is a tool, not a master. It is designed to serve us, not the other way around. The challenge lies in resisting the seductive pull of its infinite possibilities and instead wielding it with purpose. This means approaching technology not as a constant companion but as a resource to be engaged with intention and on our terms.

Imagine a life where devices enhance rather than intrude, where screens are tools for productivity, connection, or learning, not portals to distraction. In this vision, boundaries around technology are not rigid constraints but deliberate choices that prioritize presence and focus. It is a life where the dinner table is a space for conversation rather than scrolling, where the morning begins with reflection rather than a flood of notifications, and where work is a time of deep engagement rather than a series of fractured attempts to juggle tasks.

Achieving this balance requires more than individual effort; it calls for a cultural shift in how we value attention and connection. It demands that we challenge the norms of perpetual availability, questioning the assumption that faster responses and more interaction always equate to greater productivity or deeper relationships. It invites workplaces, families, and communities to foster environments that respect focus and celebrate intentionality, setting the stage for a healthier coexistence with the digital world.

At its heart, a balanced relationship with technology is about reclaiming choice. It is about deciding, moment by moment, how we want to engage with the world—whether through a screen or through the immediate and tactile experience of the present. It acknowledges that while technology is a powerful enabler, the most meaningful aspects of life—our relationships, our creativity, our sense of purpose—flourish in spaces of depth and presence.

This balance is not a static achievement but an ongoing practice, a dance between the demands of the digital age and the timeless need for connection, focus, and rest. It requires vigilance, adaptability, and a willingness to pause and reflect. But the reward is profound: a life where technology enriches rather than dominates, where our attention is spent intentionally, and where we are fully present in the moments that matter most.

Designing a Healthier

The current state of the digital landscape reflects an imbalance of power, where the interests of corporations have overshadowed the needs and well-being of individuals and society. At the core of this imbalance lies a business model that commodifies attention and prioritizes profit, perpetuating a system that thrives on user manipulation and dependency. This dynamic has led to an urgent need for systemic change—a shift from fragmented, individual attempts to mitigate harm toward collective, structural solutions that address the root causes of these issues. The conversation must extend beyond personal responsibility, challenging the pervasive narrative that users alone are to blame for their digital overindulgence. Instead, it is crucial to focus on the frameworks and structures that shape these behaviors, laying the groundwork for a reimagined relationship between technology, its creators, and its users.

Systemic change cannot be approached as a monolithic effort; it requires the coordination of multiple disciplines, perspectives, and stakeholders. Ethical tech design offers a way forward by embedding principles of transparency, autonomy, and inclusivity into the technological fabric. Regulation of algorithms emerges as a critical safeguard against unchecked power, addressing the opaque mechanisms that influence behavior and exacerbate social inequalities. Education on digital literacy equips individuals with the tools to navigate this complex landscape, empowering them to make informed decisions and demand accountability. Each of these dimensions is a vital piece of a larger puzzle, and together, they represent a cohesive response to the challenges posed by the current digital ecosystem. By addressing these elements collectively, society can begin to restore balance and foster a healthier, more equitable technological environment.

Ethical Tech Design: A Human-Centered Framework

Ethical tech design embodies the principle that technology should serve humanity, not exploit it. At its core, this approach challenges the profit-driven incentives that have dominated the development of digital platforms and tools. Rather than designing systems that maximize user engagement through addictive features, ethical design prioritizes user autonomy, well-being, and equity. This requires a deliberate shift in the design philosophy of technology companies, where the primary metric of success moves away from time spent on a platform or clicks generated and toward meaningful, positive user experiences. By placing human needs at the center of the design process, technology can become a force for empowerment rather than manipulation.

A human-centered framework begins with transparency. Users must have clear, accessible information about how their data is collected, processed, and used. This is not merely a legal obligation fulfilled through dense terms of service agreements but a genuine commitment to clarity and trust. Transparency extends to algorithmic operations, offering users insight into why they see certain content or recommendations, thereby enabling informed choices.

Equally important is the principle of designing for autonomy. Features that respect user control, such as customizable settings for notifications, time-limiting options, or straightforward data management tools, empower individuals to tailor their digital experiences to align with personal goals rather than platform-driven agendas. This contrasts sharply with the current landscape, where default settings often prioritize corporate interests and subtly nudge users toward behaviors that serve those ends.

Inclusivity forms another cornerstone of ethical design. This entails not only addressing accessibility for individuals with disabilities but also considering the diverse cultural, social, and economic contexts in which technology is used. Ethical design ensures that marginalized voices are not excluded from the digital ecosystem, whether through biased algorithms, language barriers, or systemic inequalities embedded within the technology.

Implementing such a framework requires collaboration between designers, engineers, policymakers, and ethicists, ensuring that ethical considerations are integrated at every stage of the development process. While this paradigm shift might seem ambitious, successful precedents already exist, such as platforms designed to enhance mental health rather than exacerbate it or educational apps built to foster genuine learning rather than mere gamified retention. These examples illustrate that ethical tech design is not an abstract ideal but a tangible, achievable reality that can guide the future of the digital world.

REGULATION OF ALGORITHMS: BALANCING INNOVATION WITH ACCOUNTABILITY

The regulation of algorithms represents a critical juncture in the evolution of the digital age, where unchecked innovation must meet accountability to ensure technology aligns with societal values. Algorithms, the invisible engines driving everything from search results to personalized advertisements, wield immense power over individual choices and collective behavior. Yet, their operations often remain shrouded in opacity, leaving users subject to decisions made by systems they neither understand nor control. Balancing the immense potential of algorithmic innovation with ethical and societal accountability requires a multi-faceted approach that safeguards public interest while fostering technological progress.

At the heart of this regulatory challenge lies the demand for transparency. Algorithms should not function as inscrutable black boxes but as systems open to scrutiny by users, policymakers, and independent auditors. Transparency entails providing comprehensible explanations of algorithmic logic, ensuring stakeholders can assess the fairness, accuracy, and biases embedded within these systems. However, this is not merely a technical challenge but a communicative one, requiring innovations in how complex processes are conveyed to non-technical audiences.

Accountability mechanisms are equally essential. Regulators must establish frameworks that hold organizations responsible for the societal impacts of their algorithms. This could involve creating standards for algorithmic fairness, mandating periodic audits to identify and mitigate biases, and imposing consequences for systems that perpetuate harm, whether through discrimination, misinformation, or exploitation. Such measures do not merely serve as punitive tools but act as incentives for ethical innovation, encouraging companies to design algorithms that prioritize public welfare alongside profitability.

Another critical element is user agency. Regulation should empower individuals to understand and influence how algorithms affect their lives. This could include rights to opt out of algorithmic personalization, access to tools that provide visibility into decision-making processes, or even the ability to challenge algorithmic outcomes. By embedding user rights within regulatory frameworks, society can counteract the growing asymmetry of power between individuals and the entities deploying these systems.

Collaboration between governments, private sector leaders, and civil society is indispensable to this endeavor. International cooperation will be particularly crucial, given the global nature of many algorithm-driven platforms. Establishing universal principles—such as those outlined in the emerging field of AI ethics—can help align diverse regulatory efforts while respecting regional values and norms.

The regulation of algorithms must strike a delicate balance: fostering innovation that benefits humanity while curbing the excesses that lead to exploitation, polarization, and harm. This is not a call to stifle creativity but to guide it with the understanding that technology serves its highest purpose when it enhances human dignity, equity, and collective progress. As algorithms continue to shape the contours of the digital age, ensuring their alignment with these principles will determine whether they become tools of empowerment or instruments of unchecked influence.

EDUCATION ON DIGITAL LITERACY: EMPOWERING INFORMED USERS

Education on digital literacy is pivotal in creating a society that can navigate the complexities of the digital world with autonomy and discernment. As technology increasingly infiltrates every aspect of life, from how we communicate to how we access information, a lack of understanding leaves individuals vulnerable to manipulation, misinformation, and overreliance on opaque systems. Empowering users with the skills to critically engage with technology is not merely a protective measure but a transformative one, fostering a population capable of leveraging digital tools for personal and societal advancement.

Digital literacy begins with foundational competencies: the ability to understand and interact with digital interfaces, interpret information critically, and recognize the mechanisms underpinning online platforms. Users must grasp how algorithms prioritize content, the ways in which data is collected and monetized, and the implications of these processes for privacy and autonomy. This awareness is the first step toward resisting the passive consumption of technology and reclaiming agency over digital experiences.

However, digital literacy extends beyond functional knowledge; it encompasses the cultivation of critical thinking. Users must learn to evaluate the credibility of sources, identify biases in digital content, and question the motivations of entities driving digital narratives. In an era of algorithmically amplified misinformation, the ability to distinguish fact from manipulation is essential not only for individual empowerment but also for the preservation of informed public discourse and democracy itself.

Practical application is equally important. Educational initiatives should teach users how to set boundaries with technology, manage their digital footprints, and implement tools that enhance their online security and privacy. Equipping individuals with these actionable skills transforms theoretical understanding into meaningful, everyday practices that mitigate the risks associated with digital engagement.

For digital literacy to have a widespread impact, education must begin early and persist throughout life. Schools play a crucial role in integrating digital literacy into curricula, ensuring that young people develop these skills alongside traditional academic knowledge. However, adult education programs, workplace training, and community initiatives are equally vital, addressing gaps in understanding among those who did not grow up with digital tools or whose knowledge has not kept pace with technological evolution.

The promotion of digital literacy also requires addressing systemic barriers to access and education. Economic disparities, geographic isolation, and technological divides can prevent many individuals from acquiring these essential skills. Policies and programs that ensure equitable access to digital tools and literacy resources are therefore foundational to creating a digitally informed society.

Ultimately, digital literacy is about more than navigating technology; it is about cultivating a mindset of inquiry and adaptability in a world defined by rapid technological change. Empowering users with digital literacy transforms them from passive participants in the attention economy into informed actors capable of shaping their own digital experiences. By embedding these skills at every level of society, we can ensure that technology remains a tool for empowerment rather than a source of exploitation, unlocking its potential for collective progress.

The Interconnection of Ethics, Regulation, and Education

The interplay between ethics, regulation, and education forms the backbone of a healthier digital ecosystem, with each component reinforcing the others in a synergistic relationship. Ethical technology design establishes the principles that guide innovation, ensuring that platforms and tools prioritize human well-being over profit-driven exploitation. Regulation, in turn, provides the structural framework to enforce these principles, holding companies accountable for their impact on society and mitigating the risks of unchecked technological advancement. Education bridges the gap between these systemic measures and individual empowerment, equipping users with the knowledge and skills to navigate and shape the digital world responsibly.

Ethical tech design cannot function in isolation. While it may produce more humane technologies, its efficacy is limited without mechanisms to ensure accountability. Regulation addresses this gap, translating ethical ideals into enforceable standards that compel compliance. For example, privacy-by-design principles, while ethically sound, require legal mandates to incentivize their widespread adoption. Similarly, algorithmic transparency, a cornerstone of ethical digital systems, depends on robust regulatory oversight to prevent opaque practices that exploit users.

Conversely, regulation is incomplete without public awareness and understanding. Education ensures that individuals and communities can comprehend the significance of these regulations and advocate for their enforcement. Without an informed populace, even the most progressive regulatory frameworks risk becoming toothless, as users remain unaware of their rights or the systemic forces shaping their digital interactions. Digital literacy programs empower individuals to demand accountability, creating a feedback loop where public pressure reinforces the ethical and regulatory standards governing technology.

Ethics and education are also deeply intertwined. An ethical approach to technology design should not only prioritize user well-being but also actively support educational initiatives. Platforms that encourage critical thinking, transparency, and informed decision-making foster a culture of digital literacy. For instance, social media platforms that integrate features to identify credible sources of information or highlight data-sharing policies contribute directly to the educational process. In this sense, ethical design does not merely minimize harm but actively enhances users' capacity to engage critically with technology.

Education, in turn, informs ethical design by amplifying user voices and expectations. As individuals become more digitally literate, they can articulate their needs and concerns more effectively, influencing the priorities of technology creators. This dynamic fosters a participatory model of innovation, where user feedback shapes the ethical frameworks guiding development.

The integration of ethics, regulation, and education is crucial for addressing the systemic challenges of the attention economy. Fragmented approaches that prioritize one element at the expense of others are insufficient in tackling the complex interplay of technological, societal, and individual factors driving cognitive overload and exploitation. Only by aligning these three pillars can we create a digital environment that not only mitigates harm but also empowers users and supports collective well-being. This holistic approach transforms the digital ecosystem from a space of extraction into one of enrichment, where technology serves humanity rather than undermines it.

A CALL TO ACTION

The transformation toward a healthier digital ecosystem demands more than passive acknowledgment of the issues; it requires collective action from individuals, institutions, and industries. The power to create meaningful change lies in the hands of everyone who participates in the digital landscape, whether as developers, regulators, educators, or users. Each group holds unique responsibilities and opportunities to reshape technology's trajectory toward one that prioritizes human flourishing over unchecked exploitation.

For developers and technology companies, the call to action begins with a commitment to ethical innovation. The prioritization of user well-being must no longer be a secondary consideration or a marketing slogan; it must become a core principle embedded in every stage of the design process. This means not only eliminating exploitative features like manipulative algorithms or addictive interfaces but also envisioning new tools that foster genuine connection, creativity, and well-being. Transparency, accountability, and collaboration with independent oversight bodies should become non-negotiable standards.

Regulators must step forward to establish and enforce policies that align technological progress with societal values. The call here is not to stifle innovation but to guide it responsibly, ensuring that the benefits of digital advancements are distributed equitably and without harm. This involves creating comprehensive frameworks for algorithmic oversight, implementing penalties for data misuse, and incentivizing companies to adopt ethical practices. Policymakers must work in tandem with technologists, sociologists, and legal experts to craft regulations that are both technically feasible and socially relevant, while also remaining adaptable to future advancements.

Educators, both formal and informal, have a pivotal role in cultivating digital literacy. The call to action for this group is to create accessible, engaging, and practical resources that empower individuals to navigate the digital world critically and confidently. Schools and universities should integrate digital ethics and literacy into their curricula, while community organizations can offer workshops and resources for broader audiences. Content creators and influencers, too, have a responsibility to amplify awareness and promote constructive dialogue about technology's impact on society.

For individuals, the call to action begins with introspection and personal responsibility. Users must recognize their agency in shaping digital dynamics through the choices they make daily—what they click, share, and consume. Small, intentional actions, such as supporting ethical platforms, advocating for stronger protections, or mentoring others in digital literacy, collectively contribute to systemic change. Beyond personal habits, individuals have the power to demand better from the institutions and companies that govern the digital ecosystem. Public advocacy, informed voting, and grassroots movements can exert pressure for reform, signaling that the era of exploitation must give way to one of mutual respect and sustainability.

The urgency of this call lies in the consequences of inaction. Without deliberate efforts to redesign our relationship with technology, the harms of cognitive overload, social fragmentation, and exploitation will continue to intensify. Yet, the potential for transformation is immense. By embracing this call to action, society can reclaim agency, foster innovation that aligns with human values, and build a digital future that serves as a force for collective progress rather than division. The journey requires vision, collaboration, and persistence, but the reward—a more equitable, thoughtful, and empowering digital world—is well worth the effort.

The Emergence of Counter-Movements

The emergence of counter-movements in response to the overwhelming dominance of the attention economy signals a pivotal shift in societal consciousness. As digital platforms became ever more entrenched in daily life, voices began to emerge advocating for a reevaluation of their impact. These movements are not reactionary but deeply reflective, questioning the ethical frameworks—or lack thereof—that have allowed technological innovation to outpace considerations of its effects on human cognition, relationships, and well-being. At their core, these counter-movements arise from a collective realization that the unbridled pursuit of attention commodification has led to unintended yet profound consequences, including cognitive overload, societal polarization, and diminished agency in users' lives. By identifying the systemic nature of these problems, counter-movements have sought to address them through a combination of advocacy, education, and practical reform initiatives.

One of the defining features of these counter-movements is their focus on recalibrating the relationship between technology and its users. This recalibration does not simply aim to mitigate harm; rather, it envisions a more balanced and equitable digital landscape where technology serves humanity rather than exploits it. Advocates argue that the current trajectory of technological design prioritizes profit over people, resulting in products optimized to capture attention at the expense of mental health and social cohesion. Counter-movements bring attention to this imbalance, calling for a realignment of priorities. This realignment is not merely theoretical; it requires the active participation of technologists, policymakers, and end-users, each of whom has a role in fostering a healthier dynamic between innovation and ethical responsibility.

Crucially, these movements emphasize the systemic roots of the problem, highlighting that individual actions—while important—cannot alone counteract the pervasive influence of the attention economy. Instead, they advocate for collective action and structural change. By identifying the interplay between corporate practices, regulatory frameworks, and cultural norms, counter-movements make the case for a multi-pronged approach to reform. This systemic lens also underscores the limitations of purely technological fixes, such as app timers or productivity tools, which address symptoms rather than causes. The counter-movements urge a deeper examination of the economic and psychological mechanisms driving exploitative design, proposing systemic solutions that are preventative rather than reactive.

These movements also draw from historical parallels to contextualize their efforts, often invoking lessons from previous periods of technological disruption. For instance, the rise of industrialization brought about labor reforms and workplace safety standards, which emerged only after society acknowledged the costs of unregulated innovation. Similarly, countermovements in the digital age argue that the ethical design of technology is not an optional consideration but a necessary evolution. They frame their work as part of a broader arc of progress, one in which humanity consistently seeks to balance the benefits of technological advancement with the imperatives of human dignity, autonomy, and well-being. By situating their advocacy within this historical context, they aim to garner broader support for their vision of a more humane and sustainable digital future.

Overview of the "Slow Tech" Movement

The "slow tech" movement has emerged as a deliberate counterbalance to the rapid and often unreflective pace of technological innovation. At its core, the movement seeks to reimagine the development and usage of technology, prioritizing mindfulness, ethical design, and sustainable practices over relentless growth and optimization. Inspired by the principles of the broader "slow movement," which emphasizes intentionality and quality in areas like food, travel, and living, slow tech advocates argue for a measured approach to digital tools that values long-term well-being over short-term convenience. This ethos extends beyond individual use, calling for a cultural and systemic shift in how technology is conceived, implemented, and integrated into daily life.

The slow tech philosophy begins with the premise that technology, while transformative, should enhance human lives without diminishing the very qualities that make us human. Proponents criticize the prevailing industry culture, which often prioritizes speed, novelty, and profitability, for fostering products that exploit attention, encourage overuse, and compromise mental health. Slow tech, in contrast, envisions a design framework where the user's well-being is paramount. This includes building tools that respect cognitive and emotional boundaries, fostering focus rather than distraction, and ensuring that technology serves as a complement to human capacities rather than a replacement. In this way, the movement seeks to address not just the effects of harmful technology but also its root causes by rethinking the incentives that drive its creation.

A key element of the movement involves advocating for practices that enable individuals and organizations to engage with technology more intentionally. Slow tech champions suggest strategies like digital minimalism, where users carefully curate their digital environments to focus on what truly adds value to their lives. This includes reducing unnecessary apps, limiting screen time, and emphasizing high-quality digital interactions over quantity. Additionally, the movement encourages a reevaluation of metrics used to gauge success in the tech industry, proposing that companies measure impact not in terms of engagement or revenue but in terms of user satisfaction, ethical integrity, and societal benefit. Such a redefinition of success aligns with the broader goals of the movement, fostering a healthier relationship between society and its technological tools.

Beyond individual practices, the slow tech movement engages with broader societal and systemic challenges. It calls for more transparent governance of technology development, urging policymakers to enact regulations that align innovation with public good. Advocates often collaborate with educators, nonprofits, and designers to promote digital literacy, ethical standards, and sustainability within the tech sector. By focusing on these collective efforts, the movement underscores its belief that meaningful change requires not just personal responsibility but also a reimagining of the systems that shape our digital lives. In its pursuit of balance, the slow tech movement offers a compelling vision of progress, one that embraces technological advancement while safeguarding the values of intentionality, equity, and human flourishing.

SPOTLIGHT ON HUMANE TECHNOLOGY ADVOCACY

Humane technology advocacy has emerged as a powerful force in reshaping the ethical landscape of digital innovation, striving to align technological development with human values and societal well-being. At its heart, this movement addresses the often-overlooked question: *What is technology for?* By re-centering the conversation around human dignity, autonomy, and flourishing, advocates seek to challenge the exploitative practices of tech giants that prioritize profit and engagement metrics over user welfare. This form of advocacy is not merely reactive but also profoundly visionary, proposing actionable frameworks for creating technology that respects psychological, emotional, and cognitive boundaries while fostering community and connection.

One of the most influential groups driving this movement is the Center for Humane Technology (CHT), an organization founded by former tech insiders disillusioned with the industry's current trajectory. CHT has played a pivotal role in raising public awareness about the ways technology can manipulate human behavior, from fostering compulsive use to amplifying divisiveness and misinformation. Through campaigns, research, and policy recommendations, the organization underscores the need for systemic change, advocating for design principles that promote intentional use and transparency. CHT's efforts have also led to partnerships with educational institutions and policymakers, highlighting the urgent need for cross-sector collaboration to address the societal consequences of unregulated technological growth.

In parallel, other organizations and movements are complementing this advocacy by addressing specific dimensions of humane technology. For instance, the Time Well Spent initiative focuses on creating tools and interfaces that prioritize quality over quantity in user engagement, aiming to design systems that leave people feeling fulfilled rather than drained. Similarly, the Digital Wellness Collective connects educators, technologists, and mental health professionals to foster a multidisciplinary approach to designing healthier tech ecosystems. These initiatives recognize that change requires a holistic strategy, combining ethical design, user empowerment, and regulatory oversight to create a sustainable digital future.

Humane technology advocacy also recognizes the importance of equipping individuals with the skills and knowledge necessary to navigate an increasingly complex digital environment. Efforts in this domain often emphasize the development of digital literacy programs, which teach critical skills such as discerning reliable information, understanding algorithmic biases, and recognizing the psychological tactics used in tech design. Advocates argue that an informed user base is essential for sustaining the movement's goals, as individuals must be empowered to demand greater accountability from both industry leaders and policymakers. By fostering this dual focus on systemic reform and individual agency, humane technology advocacy offers a comprehensive and hopeful pathway for addressing the profound challenges posed by today's digital landscape.

CORE STRATEGIES AND PHILOSOPHIES

At the heart of humane technology advocacy lie core strategies and philosophies that seek to redefine the relationship between humans and technology, moving from exploitation toward empowerment. These strategies rest on a fundamental philosophy: that technology should serve humanity, not the reverse. This guiding principle challenges the prevailing design ethos of maximizing screen time and engagement at the expense of user well-being, instead promoting a vision where technology enriches life rather than detracting from it. The movement's strategies are diverse, encompassing design reform, education, and systemic accountability, all underpinned by a commitment to ethical and sustainable innovation.

One critical strategy is the promotion of "human-centered design," which prioritizes the psychological, emotional, and social needs of users over metrics like clicks, views, or revenue generation. Advocates call for the elimination of addictive features, such as infinite scrolling and intermittent reward mechanisms, which exploit cognitive vulnerabilities. Instead, they champion tools that encourage mindful usage, such as screen time limits, notifications that foster intentional engagement, and interfaces designed to reduce distraction. This approach integrates insights from behavioral psychology and neuroscience, emphasizing the importance of aligning technology with natural human rhythms and cognitive capacities.

Another key philosophy is the concept of "digital dignity," which reframes users not as mere consumers but as individuals deserving of respect, agency, and privacy. This principle underpins strategies aimed at enhancing user transparency, such as clearly communicating how algorithms work and offering tools for customization. By empowering users to take control of their digital experiences, advocates argue that technology can become a means of self-expression and connection, rather than a source of stress or manipulation. This philosophy also addresses issues of equity, recognizing that vulnerable populations are often disproportionately affected by exploitative digital practices and pushing for inclusive solutions that ensure fair access and representation.

Collaboration is another cornerstone strategy, as advocates recognize that no single entity can address the multifaceted challenges of creating a humane digital ecosystem. This philosophy encourages partnerships across sectors, bringing together technologists, psychologists, educators, and policymakers to foster innovation while establishing guardrails. For instance, coalitions advocating for algorithmic accountability work with regulators to develop frameworks that ensure algorithms are not only transparent but also aligned with ethical standards. Similarly, alliances with educators focus on integrating digital literacy into school curricula, equipping future generations with the tools to navigate the complexities of a digital-first world.

Ultimately, these core strategies and philosophies aim to strike a balance between innovation and accountability, recognizing that technology's power to transform society is both its greatest strength and its greatest risk. By advocating for a paradigm shift from profit-driven design to values-driven design, humane technology proponents envision a future where digital tools enhance human potential, strengthen communities, and contribute to a more equitable and sustainable world. This vision underscores the importance of systemic change, while remaining grounded in the practical realities of implementation, ensuring that the principles of humane technology can be both aspirational and actionable.

Impact and Influence

The impact and influence of movements advocating for humane technology and ethical design are increasingly evident across industries, governance, and public consciousness. These efforts, though still in their nascent stages, have begun to reshape how individuals, organizations, and societies view the role of technology in daily life. By challenging entrenched paradigms of profit-driven innovation and fostering awareness about the psychological and social costs of unchecked technological growth, such movements have catalyzed meaningful dialogue and incremental changes that carry the potential for long-term systemic transformation.

One significant area of influence has been the introduction of ethical considerations into corporate practices. Major technology firms, under pressure from advocacy groups and a more informed public, have started adopting measures to promote user well-being. For instance, companies have implemented features like app usage timers, focus modes, and tools for monitoring screen time. While these changes may seem superficial, they represent a shift toward acknowledging the broader implications of their products on mental health and societal cohesion. Moreover, some organizations have begun to hire ethics officers or form dedicated teams tasked with ensuring that product development aligns with humane design principles, signaling a slow but growing commitment to accountability.

Another area where these movements have left a mark is public policy. Governments and regulatory bodies, spurred by advocacy campaigns, have started to take a closer look at how technologies operate and the potential harm they may cause. Legislation aimed at protecting digital privacy, limiting algorithmic manipulation, and regulating the addictive features of apps has gained traction in multiple regions. These legal frameworks not only address immediate concerns but also lay the groundwork for future advancements in technology that prioritize human dignity and societal well-being. Movements like the "Right to Disconnect" in Europe, which seeks to limit workplace technologies' encroachment on personal time, reflect the growing influence of humane technology principles in shaping public discourse and lawmaking.

The cultural and educational realms have also felt the ripple effects of these initiatives. Schools and universities are increasingly incorporating digital literacy and ethics into their curricula, recognizing that the next generation of tech users and developers must be equipped to navigate and shape a humane digital landscape. Documentaries, books, and media campaigns have brought issues like algorithmic bias, data privacy, and tech addiction to the forefront of public awareness, sparking critical conversations about the role of technology in modern life. The influence of these narratives has cultivated a sense of urgency and personal responsibility, encouraging individuals to reflect on their own technology habits and demand more ethical practices from the companies they support.

Despite these achievements, the road ahead remains fraught with challenges. The influence of humane technology advocacy is often countered by the sheer scale of profit-driven motivations within the tech industry, where the economic incentives to maximize engagement often outweigh ethical considerations. However, the growing demand for change—evident in grassroots movements, corporate shifts, and legislative efforts—signals that the conversation has reached a tipping point. The impact of these movements lies not only in the tangible changes they have brought about but also in the values they have instilled: a collective recognition of the need to realign technological progress with the fundamental principles of human well-being and societal equity. Through continued efforts, these movements hold the potential to drive a deeper, more enduring transformation in the digital age.

Critiques and Limitations

While movements advocating for humane technology and ethical design have garnered substantial attention and support, they are not without their critiques and limitations. As with any systemic reform initiative, these movements face challenges that stem from both their structural constraints and the broader technological and economic environment in which they operate. Understanding these critiques is essential for contextualizing their impact and for identifying the gaps that must be addressed to achieve meaningful and lasting change.

One prominent critique of these movements is their reliance on voluntary adoption by technology companies. Much of the progress touted by proponents, such as screen time monitors or algorithms that prioritize user well-being, often hinges on companies' willingness to self-regulate. However, critics argue that voluntary compliance frequently leads to superficial changes designed more for public relations than for substantive reform. Initiatives like focus modes or usage tracking features may serve as a façade, diverting attention from deeper structural issues such as data exploitation or algorithmic manipulation. Without external accountability mechanisms, these movements risk being co-opted by the very entities they aim to reform.

Another limitation arises from the uneven accessibility of the principles and tools advocated by these movements. Digital literacy education and awareness campaigns are often concentrated in wealthier nations and urban centers, leaving behind populations that are most vulnerable to exploitative technologies. For example, users in developing countries, who are rapidly adopting digital platforms, may lack the resources or knowledge to demand or benefit from humane technology practices. This disparity creates a digital ethics divide, where the benefits of reform remain unevenly distributed, perpetuating global inequalities. Critics also point out that focusing primarily on individual responsibility, such as encouraging users to monitor their screen time, may inadvertently shift attention away from the systemic nature of the problem.

Economic and structural inertia within the technology industry further complicates these movements' ambitions. The business models of many tech companies are deeply entrenched in practices that prioritize engagement and profit over ethics. These models are driven by algorithms optimized for attention retention, which is fundamentally at odds with humane technology principles. Critics contend that systemic change requires a fundamental overhaul of these profit structures, a task that may be beyond the reach of advocacy groups or even regulatory bodies. The sheer scale of the technology sector and its influence on global economies makes it difficult to implement reforms that could potentially disrupt revenue streams or market dynamics.

Additionally, some detractors argue that the movements themselves may lack sufficient cohesion and a unified vision. Advocacy for humane technology encompasses a broad spectrum of goals, from algorithmic transparency to digital detox practices, leading to fragmented efforts that dilute their overall impact. Without a centralized framework or coordinated strategy, these movements may struggle to present a compelling alternative to the status quo. Furthermore, their reliance on funding from philanthropic organizations or even tech companies themselves raises concerns about potential conflicts of interest and the sustainability of their efforts over the long term.

Despite these critiques, the limitations of humane technology advocacy should not be viewed as insurmountable barriers but rather as opportunities for reflection and growth. Recognizing these challenges invites a deeper interrogation of the systemic forces that shape technology use and underscores the need for multifaceted approaches that combine grassroots action, regulatory reform, and global collaboration. By addressing these limitations, these movements can evolve to more effectively confront the complexities of the digital age and continue their pursuit of a technology ecosystem that serves humanity rather than exploits it.

FUTURE PROSPECTS AND SYNERGIES

The future of humane technology advocacy lies in its ability to evolve and synergize with parallel movements, emerging technologies, and global policy frameworks. As the digital age matures, opportunities to embed ethical principles into the foundation of technological development have become increasingly viable. By leveraging advances in artificial intelligence, decentralized systems, and collaborative governance, these movements can broaden their influence and create sustainable, systemic change. Exploring these prospects highlights both the promise and the challenges of building a more humane digital ecosystem.

One promising avenue for the future involves deeper integration between the principles of humane technology and the growing field of artificial intelligence ethics. As AI becomes a driving force in decision-making, data analysis, and consumer-facing technologies, the alignment of ethical AI with humane technology offers a pathway for addressing broader systemic concerns. For example, embedding fairness, accountability, and transparency into machine learning algorithms can help mitigate biases and exploitative practices. Advocacy groups have begun forming partnerships with AI researchers and policymakers to ensure that future innovations prioritize human welfare over corporate gain. Such collaborations, however, require sustained effort to overcome resistance from industry leaders who may view these interventions as constraints on innovation.

Another area of potential growth lies in the convergence of humane technology principles with sustainability initiatives. The environmental impact of technology—from energy-intensive data centers to the proliferation of e-waste—has sparked global concern. Humane technology advocates are increasingly recognizing the need to address not only the psychological and social effects of technology but also its environmental footprint. Synergies with movements like the Green New Deal or the circular economy could provide a comprehensive framework that integrates ethical design with sustainable practices. Efforts to create longer-lasting devices, promote repairability, and reduce digital waste can align with humane technology's broader goal of minimizing harm and maximizing benefits.

At a societal level, fostering synergies with global governance initiatives holds significant potential. International frameworks like the United Nations' Sustainable Development Goals (SDGs) or the European Union's Digital Services Act offer platforms for embedding humane technology principles into policy. These initiatives provide mechanisms for scaling efforts beyond national borders, addressing disparities in digital literacy, and holding multinational corporations accountable for unethical practices. Future prospects may include the establishment of global standards for ethical technology design or the creation of international watchdog organizations that monitor compliance and advocate for reforms. However, achieving these goals will require careful negotiation to balance the diverse interests of stakeholders across different cultural, economic, and political contexts.

The grassroots dimension of humane technology advocacy also offers promising pathways for future development. Community-led initiatives, such as cooperatively managed social networks or local digital literacy programs, could serve as incubators for scalable, human-centered solutions. These grassroots efforts are particularly well-suited to addressing the digital divide and ensuring that the benefits of ethical technology are distributed equitably. By empowering local communities to take ownership of their digital ecosystems, advocates can foster resilience and innovation at the societal level. Moreover, such efforts can generate bottom-up pressure that complements top-down regulatory approaches, creating a multi-layered strategy for systemic change.

The future of humane technology advocacy ultimately hinges on its ability to build coalitions, adapt to emerging challenges, and remain responsive to the needs of diverse populations. By seeking synergies with allied movements and integrating their principles into the broader fabric of technological development, these initiatives can sustain their momentum and expand their impact. The pursuit of a healthier digital ecosystem requires a vision that extends beyond immediate reforms to encompass a holistic reimagining of the role technology plays in human life. In doing so, the movement can inspire a global shift toward technology that prioritizes well-being, equity, and sustainability over profit and exploitation.

THE PATH FORWARD

The path forward for humane technology advocacy lies in the delicate balance between pragmatic action and visionary reform. As technology continues to shape every facet of modern life, the movement must evolve from raising awareness to implementing transformative solutions that bridge ideals with practice. This requires a multifaceted approach that embraces technological innovation, policy reform, and cultural shifts while maintaining a clear focus on the human values at the core of the movement.

One critical step is the institutionalization of humane technology principles across industries and sectors. This involves not only integrating these ideals into corporate frameworks but also embedding them into educational curricula and public policy. For example, universities could offer specialized programs in ethical technology design, fostering a generation of engineers, designers, and policymakers equipped to prioritize human-centric approaches. Governments, in turn, could create funding mechanisms that incentivize the development of technologies aligned with ethical standards. These initiatives, while ambitious, are essential to ensuring that humane technology principles become more than aspirational goals—they must be woven into the fabric of the systems that drive technological progress.

Collaboration between stakeholders is another cornerstone of the path forward. Advocacy groups, governments, academic institutions, and technology companies must work together to address complex issues that no single entity can resolve alone. Joint efforts to establish ethical benchmarks, develop robust regulatory frameworks, and share best practices are key to sustaining the momentum of humane technology. For instance, international alliances like the Global Partnership on Artificial Intelligence could serve as models for broader coalitions dedicated to humane technology. Such collaborations must also remain vigilant against the co-opting of their objectives by entities that prioritize profit over principle, ensuring that their mission is not diluted by competing interests.

Cultural transformation is equally vital in shaping the path ahead. The societal embrace of technological convenience and constant connectivity has created deeply ingrained behaviors and expectations that humane technology advocates must challenge. Shifting cultural narratives away from the glorification of hyper-productivity and endless innovation toward a focus on balance, mindfulness, and human well-being is no small task. Storytelling, media campaigns, and influential voices in art and culture can play pivotal roles in reimagining the public's relationship with technology. Empowering individuals to make conscious choices about their digital habits, supported by accessible tools and resources, can gradually foster a more mindful tech culture.

The path forward also demands an openness to reimagine and redefine what progress means in the digital age. For too long, technological advancement has been equated with the relentless pursuit of faster, more efficient, and more profitable systems. Humane technology advocates must champion a broader, more inclusive vision of progress—one that prioritizes equity, sustainability, and the flourishing of all people. This redefinition is particularly urgent in addressing global disparities, ensuring that the benefits of ethical technology reach marginalized communities and underserved populations. Innovations in affordable access, inclusive design, and localized solutions can help bridge the digital divide and promote global equity.

The movement's success hinges on its ability to inspire a collective commitment to a shared vision of technology that serves humanity rather than exploiting it. By fostering resilience, adaptability, and collaboration, humane technology advocacy can navigate the challenges ahead while staying true to its mission. The path forward is not without obstacles, but it is imbued with the potential for profound and lasting change. In charting this course, the movement offers a compelling invitation to rethink our relationship with technology and to envision a future where digital innovation is not an end in itself but a means to a more humane and equitable world.

Discover more

Autor

Other books